1947

50

1997

Motorbooks International
Publishers & Wholesalers ®

This edition first published in 1997 by Motorbooks International Publishers & Wholesalers,
729 Prospect Avenue, PO Box 1, Osceola, WI 54020 USA

© 1997 - Giorgio Nada Editore srl

Previously Published by Giorgio Nada Editore srl,
Via Claudio Treves 15/17, 20090 Vimodrone (MI), Italy

Library of Congress Cataloging-in-Publication Data Available.

ISBN 0-7603-0454-8

Printed and bound in Italy

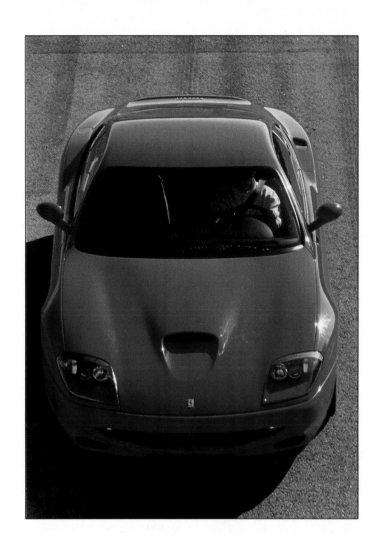

C O N T E N T S

1947

THE BIRTH OF A LEGEND

1956

*I*n the immediate po-
st-war years Enzo
Ferrari was able to
abandon the produc-
tion of machine tools
such as grinders and
milling machines and
concentrate on the re-
construction of the Ma-
ranello factory and the
production of racing
cars. To this end he cal-
led on the talents of
Gioachino Colombo
who designed the first
car, the 125, named af-
ter the individual cylin-
der capacity of its

1,500cc V-12 engine.
The car made its debut
at the Piacenza circuit
on the 11th of May,
1947. During the cour-
se of that year the total
displacement was in-
creased to 1,900cc
(159 S) and 1948 saw
the debut of the two-li-
tre engine (166) which
brought the Ferrari na-
me to world-wide atten-
tion thanks to victories
in that year's Mille Mi-
glia and the Le Mans
24 Hours in 1949. The
team's Formula 1 ventu-
res were not so imme-
diately successful. After
having started off with
the 1,500cc superchar-
ged engine, Ferrari de-
cided that the large di-
splacement, naturally
aspirated route was the
way to go in an attempt
to compete with the all-
conquering Alfa Ro-
meos. The 375 F1 desi-
gned by Aurelio Lam-
predi defeated the Al-
fas for the first time at
the British G.P. in
1951. From that mo-
ment Lampredi's Ferra-
ris became the cars to
beat in both the Formu-
la and Sports catego-
ries. Production was,
however, still on a very
limited scale. It was not
until 1952 that the firm
began its collaboration
with Pininfarina that al-
lowed it to compete
successfully on the GT
market and produce a
total of 81 cars in
1956.

1947

The Forlì circuit (6th of July):
Tazio Nuvolari, at the wheel of the
Ferrari 125 S Competizione, led the
Maranello team to its fifth success
in less than two months.

Four views of Ing. Gioacchino
Colombo's design for the
Ferrari 125 Sport.

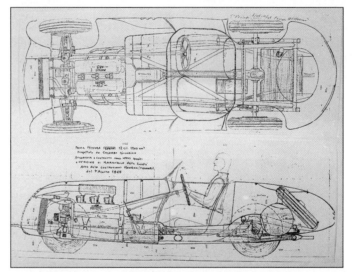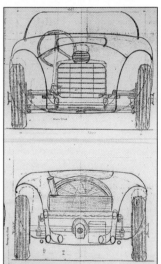

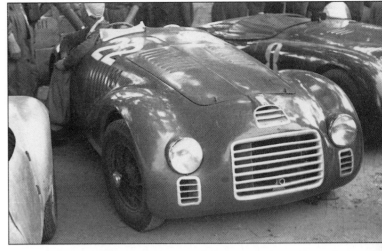

Cars	Ferrari 125 S
	Engine: V-12 1496.7cc
	Power output: 119 hp at 7000 rpm
	Ferrari 159 S
	Engine: V-12 1902cc
	Power output: 125 hp at 7000 rpm
Victories:	GP of Rome	F. Cortese
	Circuito di Forlì	T. Nuvolari
	Circuito di Pescara	F. Cortese
	Circuito di Turin	R. Sommer
	Circuito di Vercelli	F. Cortese
	Circuito di Vigevano	F. Cortese
	Circuito di Varese	N. Righetti
	Circuito di Parma	T. Nuvolari
Production:	A total of 3 examples of the 125 raced by works drivers. Out of them, one was transformed into the 159 S

Above: left, on its debut at Pescara on the 15th of August, Franco Cortese drove the Ferrari 159 S to second place overall; right, Cortese had already scored a peremptory victory at Vercelli on the 1st of June with the 125 S. Below, left, the start of the Circuito delle Cascine on the 20th of July. The 125 S on the front row of the grid was driven by Cortese and Nando Righetti and replaced the indisposed Tazio Nuvolari and his Tipo Competizione. Below, right, the rolling chassis of the 125 S takes to the road for the first time on the 12th of March with the engineer Luigi Bazzi at the wheel.

1948

The Righetti-Bruni 166 S Allemano (B. Sterzi) at the start of the 15th edition of the Mille Miglia (2nd of May). Following its triumph in the 8th Giro di Sicilia (3rd/4th of April) with the Biondetti-Troubetskoy pairing, this car was forced to retire and victory went to the Biondetti-Navone 166 S Allemano.

Above, the Mantova circuit (13th of June); Tazio Nuvolari, at the wheel of the short chassis Ferrari 166, makes his way to the starting grid accompanied by Giuseppe Navone. He was to retire due to illness. Right, a cut-away drawing of the engine.

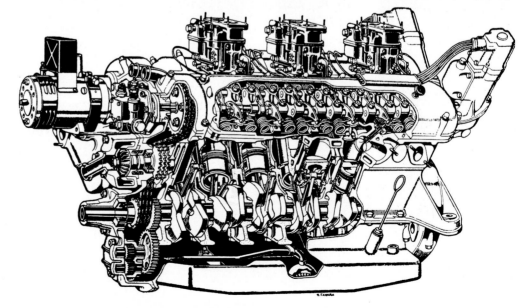

The Besana brothers at the start of
the 15th edition of the Mille Miglia
with the 166 SC. They also retired
after having passed Rome. Below,
Tazio Nuvolari talking with Enzo
Ferrari during tech inspection. The
Flying Mantuan drove an epic race,
cut short by suspension failure.

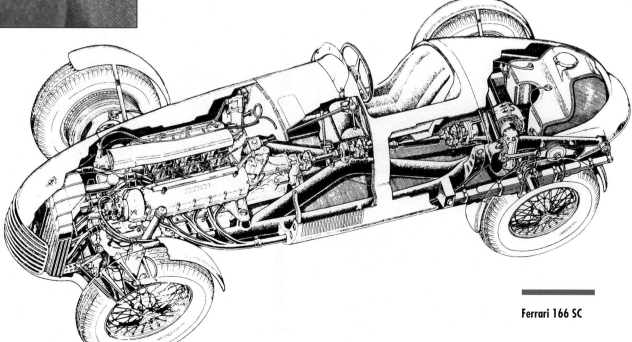

Ferrari 166 SC

9

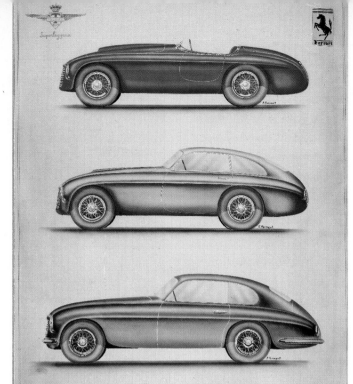

Above, two views of the 166 MM
Lusso barchetta bodied by Touring
and, top right, drawings of the three
Touring versions of the 166.

Grand Prix Cars	Ferrari 125 S	
	Engine: V-12 1498cc, compressor	
	Power output: 230 hp at 7000 rpm	
	Ferrari 166 S	
	Engine: V-12 1995cc	
	Power output: 140 hp at 6600 rpm	
Drivers:	R. Sommer, G. Farina, B. Bira, F. Cortese,	
	J. Pola, B. Sterzi	
Victories:	Circuito del Garda	G. Farina
Sports Cars	Ferrari 166 MM	
	Engine: V-12 1995cc	
	Power output: 120 hp at 6600 rpm	
Victories:	Giro di Sicilia	Trubetzkoy-Biondetti
	Mille Miglia	Biondetti-Navone
	Paris 12 Hours	L. Chinetti
Production	166 Corsa	
	166 Inter	
	166 S	

The rolling chassis of the Ferrari 166
Inter as penned by the well known
draughtsman Giovanni Cavara.

Ferrari presented its first true Formula racers in 1949. Above, the F2 Ferrari 166s driven by Felice Bonetto (No. 38) and Alberto Ascari running together during the Autodromo Grand Prix at Monza (26th of June) won by Fangio with another 166 F2. The supercharged 125 F1 was developed for Formula 1 races and the new version with twin superchargers and four overhead camshafts won the Italian Grand Prix (11th of September) in the hands of Ascari.

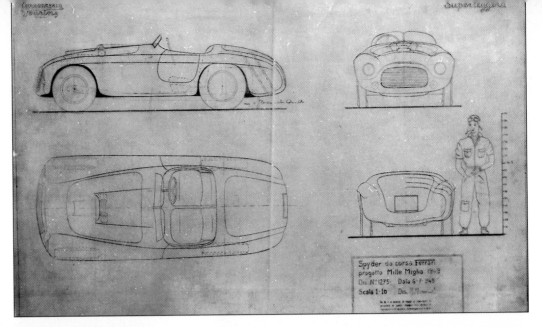

The Ferrari 166 MM (right, in a contemporary drawing) dominated sports car racing, the Tuscan driver Biondetti taking both the Giro di Sicilia and the Mille Miglia (below), while Luigi Chinetti, the marque's US concessionaire, won at Le Mans.

Grands Prix	
Car	Ferrari 125 S
	Engine: V-12 1498cc, compressor
	Power output: 260 hp at 7000 rpm
	Ferrari 166 F2
	Engine: V-12 1995cc
	Power output: 155 hp at 7000 rpm
Drivers:	A. Ascari, L. Villoresi, P. Whitehead, R. Sommer, F. Bonetto, J.M. Fangio, G. Farina
Victories:	Autodromo di Monza GP (F2) J.M. Fangio
	Rosario GP G. Farina
	Swiss GP A Ascari
	Daily Express Trophy A. Ascari
	GP of Czechoslovakia P. Whitehead
	Italian GP A. Ascari
Sports Cars	Ferrari 166
	Engine: V-12 1995cc
	Power output: 140 hp at 6600 rpm
Victories:	Giro di Sicilia Biondetti-Benedetti
	Le Mans 24 Hours Chinetti-Selsdon
	Mille Miglia Biondetti-Salani
Production	166 MM, 166 Sport, 166 Inter, 166 Corsa

The 166 Inter also entered limited production and was bodied by diverse coachbuilders of the era according to the taste of the individual client. This photo shows the 166 Inter bodied by Stabilimenti Farina that Franco Cornacchia drove to third place in the Coppa Intereuropa behind Sterzi and Bianchetti's Touring- and Allemano-bodied 166s.

Ferrari abandoned supercharging in favour of large displacement engines for its F1 cars. Alberto Ascari, left, finished second at Monte Carlo (21st of May) whilst Tadini (below) took the F2 machine to fourth in the Autodrome GP (28th of May) won by Luigi Villoresi in the 166 F2.

Two versions of the 166: the Bertone cabriolet presented at the Turin Motor Show in 1951 and two photos of the Ghia coupé designed by Felice M. Boano.

1950

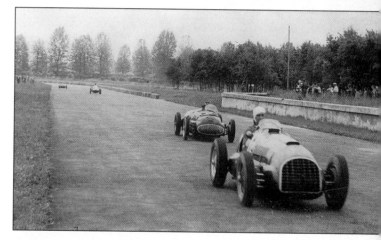

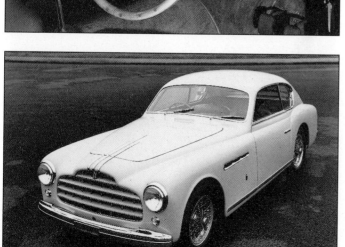

Formula 1 World Championship

Cars	Ferrari 125
	Engine: V-12 1498cc, compressor
	Power output: 260 hp at 7000 rpm
	Ferrari 275
	Engine: V-12 3322cc
	Power output: 300 hp at 7000 rpm
	Ferrari 375
	Engine: V-12 4493cc
	Power output: 350 hp at 7000 rpm
Drivers:	A. Ascari, L. Villoresi, R. Sommer, D. Serafini, P. Whitehead, C. Biondetti
Victories:	0

Sports

Cars	Ferrari 195 S	
	Engine: V-12 2341cc	
	Power output: 160 hp at 7000 rpm	
Victories:	Mille Miglia	G. Marzotto-Crosara
	Paris 12 Hours	Chinetti-Lucas
Production	166 Inter, 166 LM, 195 S, 275 S	

The Italian GP of the 16th of September revealed the full potential of the 375 F1 designed by Aurelio Lampredi. The race was won by Alberto Ascari who led home his teammate Froilan Gonzalez. Luigi Villoresi, seen here at the "Porfido" curve, finished fourth.

1951

An interesting view of Piero Taruffi's 375 F1 at the German GP (29th of July) in which he finished third behind Ascari and Gonzalez. Note the large spray-guards behind the front wheels.

Left, the victorious Alberto Ascari and his 375 F1 at the "Porfido" curve during the Italian GP.

Below, the Ferrari 375 F1 driven by Alberto Ascari at the Spanish Grand Prix held at Barcelona on the 28th of October.

Formula 1 World Championship
Cars	375 F.1	
	Engine: V-12 4493cc	
	Power output: 384 hp at 7500 rpm	
Drivers:	A. Ascari, L. Villoresi, F. Gonzales, C. Landi,	
	P. Taruffi, R. Fischer, P. Whitehead	
Victories:	British GP	F. Gonzales
	German GP	A. Ascari
	Italian GP	A. Ascari
A. Ascari	25 pts (2nd overall)	

Left, Alberto Ascari at the San Remo GP (22nd of April) held on the Ospedaletti circuit. Ascari won, favoured by the withdrawal of the Alfas, at the wheel of the twin-spark car, recognizable by the different distances between the exhaust pipes. The Milanese driver finished second in the world drivers' Championship, losing out to Fangio at the Spanish GP due to tire problems that afflicted all the 375s.

Piero Scotti finished second at Senigallia at the wheel of this 212 Export bodied by the Turinese Rocco Motto (left). The race was won by Luigi Villoresi in the Ferrari 340 spider following an in-house duel with Giannino Marzotto until the latter crashed.

In 1951 Luigi Villoresi proved to be one of the most successful Ferrari drivers, winning among other races the Mille Miglia together with Cassani. The photo right shows his Ferrari 340 America berlinetta by Vignale at the Bologna refuelling stop with the dramatic evidence of a heavy crash at Ferrara. Villoresi had also triumphed in the Coppa Intereuropa at Monza driving the same car.

The sporting activities of the Ferrari clientele continued to expand. A total of 26 Ferrari cars were entered for the 1951 Mille Miglia, 21 of which actually started. Among the 166s, behind the car of Paolo Marzotto (fourth overall), the Masseroni-Vignolo partnership (seen here at the start) distinguished itself with 21st place overall.

Sports		
Cars	Ferrari 340 America	
	Engine: V-12 4101cc	
	Power output: 230 hp at 6000 rpm	
Victories:	Giro di Sicilia	V. Marzotto-Fontana
	Mille Miglia	Villoresi-Cassani
	Carrera Panamericana	Taruffi-Chinetti
Production	212 Export	
	212 Inter	
	340 America	
	195 Inter	
	166 Inter	
	166 MM	
	166 Corsa	

Four versions cars bodied by the Carrozzeria Vignale which in those years could count on the talents of the stylist Giovanni Michelotti. Anti-clockwise from top right, the 212 Export berlinetta (chassis no. 0080E), the 195 Inter berlinetta (chassis no. 099 S), the 212 Export spider (chassis no. 0076E, formerly 006 1) and the 166 Inter berlinetta (chassis no. 0059 S7).

On the insistence of Luigi Chinetti, Ferrari entered the Indianapolis 500. Only Ascari managed to qualify, in 25th place, and retired on the 41st lap. This photo shows the Indy car driven by Giuseppe Farina at the Valentino circuit on the 6th of April.

1952

The 375 Indy cars were race tested in the Valentino GP by Ascari, Farina and Villoresi, the latter driving a version with a short wheelbase and suspension with rubber bump-stops. Right, Giuseppe Farina, the World Champion in 1950 and, below, Luigi Villoresi, the winner of the race. In the central photo, Alberto Ascari during the Italian Grand Prix at Monza on the 7th of September that saw him crowned as World Champion.

Left, the 212 spider cabriolet bodied by Ghia. Below, the 212 Inter cabriolet by Pinin Farina that marked the beginning of a prolific partnership that is still going strong. The car was produced for the Swiss enthusiast Georges Filippinetti.

Formula 1 World Championship		
Cars	500 F2	
	Engine: in-line four, 1984cc	
	Power output: 180 hp at 7200 rpm	
Drivers:	A. Ascari, G. Farina, L. Villoresi, P. Taruffi,	
	L. Rosier, P. Hirt, C. de Tornaco, R. Fischer,	
	F. Comotti, P. Carini, P. Whitehead,	
	A. Simon, R. Salvadori, R. Laurent	
Victories:	Swiss GP	P. Taruffi
	Belgian GP	A. Ascari
	French GP	A. Ascari
	British GP	A. Ascari
	German GP	A. Ascari
	Dutch GP	A. Ascari
	Italian GP	A. Ascari
A. Ascari	World Champion	
Other victories	Mille Miglia (Vignale 250 S berlinetta) Bracco-Rolfo	
Production	212 Export, 212 Inter, 225 S, 250 S, 275 S, 340 America	

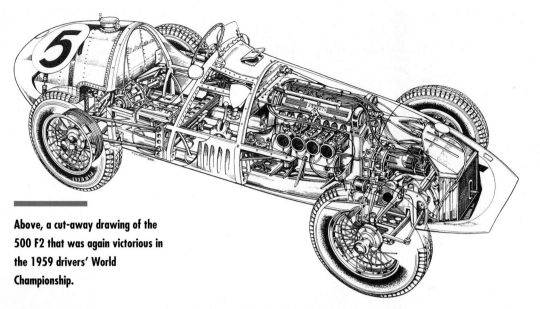

Above, a cut-away drawing of the 500 F2 that was again victorious in the 1959 drivers' World Championship.

Below, for the second year running Alberto Ascari triumphed in the World Championship. For the new racing formula introduced in 1952 and restricted to 2-litre single-seaters Aurelio Lampredi had abandoned the V-12 engine architecture in favour of an efficient in-line four. In this photo the Milanese champion on his way to victory in the A.C.F. GP at Reims (5th of July).

1953

Below, Ferrari also took the World Sports Car Championship. This photo shows Bracco and Rolfo's unfortunate new 250 MM during tech inspection for the Mille Miglia.

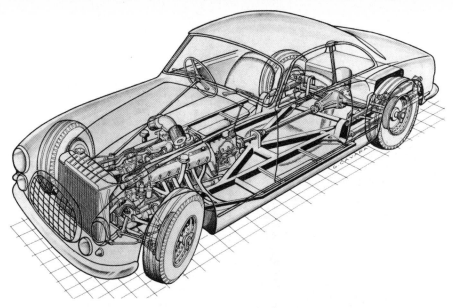

Left, as well as producing the 250 MM on the facing page and an analogous berlinetta on the 342 chassis, Pinin Farina continued to provide a coachbuilding service for non-sporting clients, creating the 212 Inter seen in this cut-away and photo. There are clear stylistic echoes of the previous year's 212 Inter cabriolet, apart from the elimination of the dummy air intakes on the bonnet. Below, a 340 America spider by Vignale ordered by Luigi Chinetti and, bottom, the Vignale 340 coupé that Luigi Mancini drove to fourth place in the Carrera Panamericana.

Formula 1 World Championship		
Cars	500 F2	
	Engine: in-line four, 1984cc	
	Power output: 180 hp at 7200 rpm	
Drivers:	A. Ascari, L. Villoresi, G. Farina, M. Hawthorn	
	L. Rosier, J. Swaters, K. Adolff, M. De Terra	
	P. Hirt, P. Carini, U. Maglioli	
Victories:	Argentine GP	A. Ascari
	Dutch GP	A. Ascari
	Belgian GP	A. Ascari
	French GP	M. Hawthorn
	British GP	A. Ascari
	German GP	G. Farina
	Swiss GP	A. Ascari
A. Ascari	World Champion	

World Sports Car Championship		
Cars	375 MM	
	Engine: V-12 4500cc, 340 hp	
Victories:	Mille Miglia	Marzotto-Crosara
	Spa 24 Hours	Hawthorn-Farina
	Nürburgring 1000 kms	Ascari-Farina
Ferrari World Sports Car Champion		
Production	250 MM,	
	342 America, 340 MM,	
	212 Inter,	
	166 MM	

The World Championship for drivers was reserved for cars with maximum displacements of 2.5 litres. Lampredi developed a car from the previous year's F2 (left) but due to the Ascari's move to Lancia and the dominance of the 6-cylinder Mercedes, Gonzales and Hawthorn only managed a single Grand Prix win each. Here the two drivers are seen in the pits during the British GP meeting (17th of July).

1954

Gonzales and Trintignant finished second in the Supercortemaggiore GP on the 27th of June (below, left) with the Scaliglietti 750. Right, the last Pinin Farina barchetta on the 735 MM chassis.

Clockwise from top right, the 375 Mille Miglia spider Le Mans, produced by Pinin Farina for Prince Boo-Dai. The Turinese coachbuilder also exhibited this 375 MM Mexico competition coupé at the Turin Motor Show, whilst the 375 America chassis formed the basis of this 2+2 with Inter styling that was also repeated in the 250 Europa cabriolet. One of the stars of the show was this 375 produced for Ingrid Bergman.

Formula 1 World Championship		
Cars	625 F1	
	Engine: in-line four, 2498cc	
	Power output: 230 hp at 7000 rpm	
Drivers:	G. Farina, F. Gonzales, M. Trintignant, M. Hawthorn,	
	J. Swaters, L. Rosier, R. Manzon, P. Taruffi, A. Ascari	
Victories:	British GP	J. F. Gonzales
	Spanish GP	M. Hawthorn
	F. Gonzales	25.5 pts (2nd overall)
	M. Hawthorn	24.5 pts (3rd overall)

World Sports Car Championship		
Cars	375 Plus	
	Engine: V-12 4954cc, 344 hp	
	750	
	Engine: in-line four, 2999cc, 260 hp	
Victories:	Buenos Aires 1000 kms	Farina-Fagioli
	Le Mans 24 Hours	Gonzales-Trintignant
	Tourist Trophy	Hawthorn-Trintignant
	Carrera Panamericana	Maglioli
Ferrari World Sports Car Champion		

Production	
	250 Europa GT
	375 S Coupé America, 375 MM, 250 MM
	250 Monza, 500 Mondial

The 4-cylinder 555 "Squalo" (left with Hawthorn in 1954) evolved into the "Supersqualo" (above) with the Lancia V-8 engine from the D50.

1955

Lampredi's four-cylinder engine was by now clearly obsolete and both the divers' and the constructors' championships were won by Mercedes. At the Supercortemaggiore GP of the 29th of May, the Hawthorn-Magioli 750 was defeated by Behra and Musso's Maserati. While testing a Ferrari at Monza Alberto Ascari was killed in a tragic accident that convinced Lancia to dismantle its racing team, ceding the D50s designed by Vittorio Jano (right, with Ascari) to Ferrari.

Ferrari had by now become the marque of kings, noblemen, magnates and show-business celebrities: below, the 375 America cabriolet created by Pinin Farina for King Leopold of Belgium.

The 250 GT Europa appeared at Paris (right and below) and introduced styling themes that were subsequently taken up for the production cars.

At the Turin Motor Show Pinin Farina presented this 375 America (above) created for Gianni Agnelli, the rear end styling of which echoed that of the car designed for Ingrid Bergman.

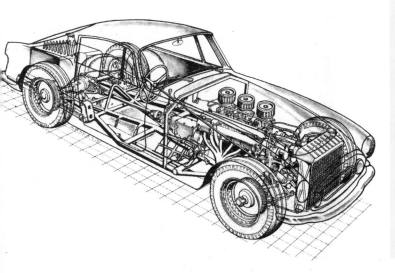

Formula 1 World Championship
Cars   555 Squalo
                Engine: in-line four, 2497cc
                Power output: 270 hp at 7500 rpm
Drivers: G. Farina, U. Maglioli, M. Trintignant, H. Schell,
                P. Taruffi, P. Frere, E. Castellotti, M. Hawthorn, J. Claes
Victories: Monaco GP   M. Trintignant
        E. Castellotti   12 pts. (3rd overall)

World Sports Car Championship
Cars   Ferrari 375 Plus
                Engine: V-12 4954cc
                Power output: 344 hp at 6500 rpm
Victories: Buenos Aires 1000 kms   Valiente-Ibanez
        Ferrari: 22 pts. (2nd overall)

Production   250 GT, 375 America, 375 MM, 750 Monza

The adoption of the Lancia racing machinery, the withdrawal of Mercedes and the signing of the three-time World Champion Juan Manuel Fangio took Ferrari back to the top in the F1 World Championship.

Ferrari also won the World Sports Car Championship. This 625 LM (right) was prepared for Le Mans and fitted with a 2.5-litre engine in accordance with the regulations restricting the engine size of prototypes.

1956

J. M. Fangio had an unfortunate Italian GP, being forced to retire on the 20th lap. His teammate Peter Collins was called into the pits and Fangio took over his car and eventually finished second behind Stirling Moss's Maserati (above). Among the most significant modifications made to the D50 was the elimination of the side-tanks in favour of a conventional single tank in the tail (right).

This 250 designed by Scaglietti (above) was homologated to race in the GT category. Enzo Ferrari with Corrado Millanta in the pits at Monza (left) two months after the death of his son Alfredo.

Formula 1 World Championship

Cars	D 50	
	Engine: V-8 2496cc	
	Power output: 230 hp at 8600 rpm	
Drivers:	J.M. Fangio, L. Musso, P. Collins, O. Gendebien,	
	E. Castellotti, G. Scarlatti, P. Frere, A. de Portago,	
	W. von Trips	
Victories:	Argentine GP	Fangio-Musso
	Belgian GP	P. Collins
	British GP	J. M. Fangio
	German GP	J. M. Fangio
J. M. Fangio		World Champion

World Sports Car Championship

Cars	290 MM	
	Engine: V-12 3490cc, 320 hp	
	860 Monza	
	Engine: in-line four, 3431cc, 350 hp	
Victories:	Sebring 12 Hours	Fangio-Castellotti
	Mille Miglia	Castellotti
	Swedish GP	Trintignant-P. Hill
Ferrari World Sports Car Champion		
Production	250 GT, 250 GT Competizione	
	410 Superamerica, 500 TR, 375 MM	

The Superfast 1, the first dream car created by Pinin Farina on the 410 Superamerica chassis (left), was dramatically different to the European-style 410 Superamerica and 250 GT (below).

1957

TOWARDS AN INDUSTRIAL SCALE

1966

*T*he 665 Ferraris constructed in 1965 represent a clear indication of the efforts made by Maranello to carve itself a niche in the automotive market, especially when compared with the total of 113 cars built up to the beginning of the decade. In order to achieve this expansion Ferrari began to produce various cars in series, all equipped with three-litre, V-12 engines with single overhead camshafts per bank and bodies by Pininfarina. While still pedigree, high-performance machinery, these cars were more driveable and comfortable than the competition models. The creators of this transformation were Carlo Chiti (under whose direction Ferrari won the Formula 1 World Championship in 1958 and 1961 and the Sports Car Championship in 1958, 1960 and 1961) and then, following Chiti's move to ATS, Mauro Forghieri, the designer of all the competition Ferrari's produced up to the mid-eighties.

After the break-down of a planned agreement with Ford in 1963, in 1965 Ferrari established contacts with the Fiat universe due to a Formula 2 regulation that specified the use of an engine derived from a car produced in at least 500 examples per year. This led to the conception and birth of the Fiat Dino powered by a V-6 power plant, with the same unit being used in the Ferrari 206 GT that appeared in 1967. This was the first mid-engined production Ferrari, a layout that had been adopted for the firm's competition machines since 1960-61.

1957

Top, the arrival of Piero Taruffi's 315S, winner of the last Mille Miglia. De Portago's tragic accident at Guidizzolo with the 335 S marked the end of the great Italian endurance race. Tragedy had already struck the Maranello firm with the loss of Eugenio Castellotti at the Modena circuit on the 14th of March. The F1 car still used the Lancia V-8 engine whilst the new 1500 cc F2 (above) used the brand-new Dino V-6 unit that Dino Ferrari himself had helped to design.

Ferrari offered the 500 TRC to private entrants. This car was built to category C regulations which specified that a hood had to be fitted (right). The Ferrari clientele were particularly taken with Scaglietti's 250 GT California (below), inspired by the Pininfarina cabriolet presented at the Frankfurt Motor Show (below).

Formula 1 World Championship	
Cars	D 50 - Engine: V-8 2496cc
	Power output: 231 hp at 8600 rpm
Drivers:	F. Gonzales, A. De Portago, W. von Trips,
	L. Musso, C. Perdisa, P. Collins, M. Hawthorn,
	E. Castellotti, A. De Tomaso, M. Trintignant,
L. Musso	15 pts (3rd overall)

World Sports Car Championship		
Cars	290 MM - Engine: V-12 3490cc, 350 hp	
	335 S - Engine: V-12 4023cc, 390 hp	
Victories:	Buenos Aires 1000 kms	Gregory-Perdisa-Musso-Castellotti
	GP of Venezuela	P. Hill-Collins
	Mille Miglia	P. Taruffi
World Sports Car Champions		

Production	500 TRC, 250 GT, 250 GT Competizione,
	410 Superamerica, 410 Superfast, 290 MM

1958

Tragedy struck yet again with the loss of the English driver Peter Collins (left) at the Nürburgring on the 3rd of August, and Luigi Musso (bottom, left) at Reims on the 6th of July. The World Championship was won by the consistent Mike Hawthorn, portrayed here a few years earlier on a Lambretta (below, right).

The reduction of the maximum cylinder capacity for Sports Cars to 3000 cc placed Ferrari in a position of strength with respects to Aston Martin and Jaguar who were left without suitable engines. The Ferrari 250 Testa Rossa equipped with a V-12 engine derived from the production unit was triumphant.

Increasing attention was paid to the production of GT road cars. After the threshold of 100 cars per year had been reached for the first time in 1957, Ferrari built almost 200 in 1958. The best seller was the new 250 GT coupé by Pininfarina (right). Pininfarina presented this elegant car based on the 410 SA chassis at Paris. It was similar to the coupé produced for Liliana de Réthy (below).

The racing activities of the privateers were revitalised with the presentation of the Scaglietti berlinetta known as the Tour de France in honour of Gendebien and Bianchi's success in that race. Below, the berlinettas on the starting grid for the Coppa Intereuropa

Formula 1 World Championship

Cars	246 F1	
	Engine: V- 6 2417cc	
	Power output: 250 hp at 8300 rpm	
Drivers:	L. Musso, M. Hawthorn, P. Collins, W. von Trips	
	O. Gendebien	
Victories:	French GP	M. Hawthorn
	Glover Trophy	M. Hawthorn
	Syracuse GP	L. Musso
M. Hawthorn	World Champion	
Ferrari	40 pts (2nd, Constructors' Championship)	

World Sports Car Championship

Cars	250 Testa Rossa	
	Engine: V-12 2953cc	
	Power output: 300 hp at 7200 rpm	
Victories:	Buenos Aires 1000 kms	P. Hill-Collins
	Sebring 12 Hours	P. Hill-Collins
	Targa Florio	Musso-Gendebien
World Sports Car Champions		

Production	250 GT, 250 GT Competizione, 410 Superamerica, 250 GT 2 seater Pininfarina, 250 GT Spider California, 250 Testa Rossa

ARight, The American Phil Hill chasing his team-mate Tony Brooks during the French GP at Reims on the 5th of July. Hill eventually finished second.

1959

The most significant innovation for 1959 was the adoption of Dunlop disc brakes. Above, Tony Brooks in the 246 with Phil Hill sitting on the wheel at Monza in June. The 250 TR lost the sports car championship to the Aston Martins in spite of the victory at Sebring where Jean Behra (above right) also finished second. Right a cut-away drawing of the 250 TR.

Formula 1 World Championship		
Cars	246	
	Engine: V-6 2474cc	
	Power output: 280 hp at 8500 rpm	
Drivers:	J. Behra, T. Brooks, P. Hill, C. Allison, D. Gurney,	
	O. Gendebien, W. von Trips	
Victories:	French GP	T. Brooks
	Aintree GP	J. Behra
T. Brooks	27 pts (2nd overall)	
Ferrari	32 pts (2nd, FIA Constructor's Championship)	

Other competition cars

250 Testa Rossa Sport
Engine: V-12 2953cc, 300 hp
156 F2
Engine: V-6 1476cc, 150 hp

Production   250 GT, 250 GT Competizione,
250 Spider California, 410 Superamerica

Two special Pininfarina bodies: a 250 GT presented at Geneva and the 410 built for Gianni Agnelli (left).

Top, the technical staff testing the 250 TR at Modena with Jean Behra. Marchetti, Tavoni and Ingegnere Chiti can all be recognised.

The adoption of disc brakes the previous year and an increase in power output were not sufficient to defeat the rear-engined English cars. The Ferraris' only victory was in the Italian GP deserted by the English teams. On the left, von Trips' F2 tailing Mairesse.

1960

Following the debut at Monte Carlo of a rear-engined 246 driven by Ginther, Ferrari dedicated itself to preparation for the 1961 championship to be run for cars with 1500 cc engines. The 156 P made its debut at Monza on the 4th of September with von Trips.

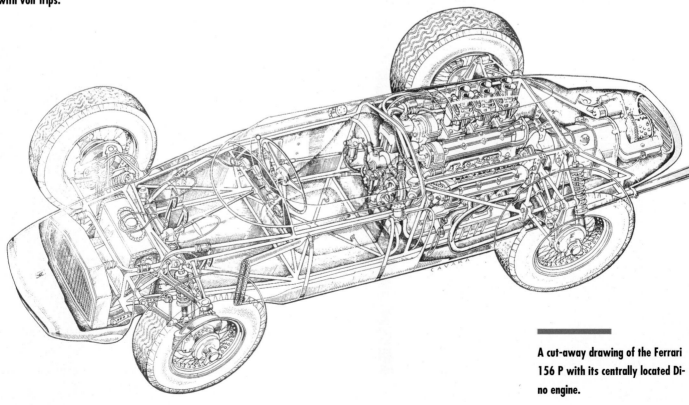

A cut-away drawing of the Ferrari 156 P with its centrally located Dino engine.

Alongside the Pininfarina creations, other coachbuilders also bodied the Ferrari chassis. Right, the 250 GT designed by Giorgetto Giugiaro and produced by Bertone who exhibited it at the Geneva Motor Show. At the Turin show Pininfarina presented the latest of its dream car styling exercises, the Superfast II on a 400 SA chassis (below).

Presented at the 1959 Paris Motor Show, the Scaglietti berlinetta adopted a shorter wheelbase in 1960 and was produced with aluminium panelling for competition and as a steel-bodied Gran Turismo.

Formula 1 World Championship		
Cars	246 e 156 P	
	Engine (246): V-6 2417cc	
	Power output: 280 hp at 9000 rpm	
Drivers:	C. Allison, W. von Trips, P. Hill, R. Ginther,	
	F. Gonzales, W. Mairesse	
Victories:	Italian GP	P. Hill
Ferrari	26 pts. (3rd, Constructors' World Championship)	
World Sports Car Championship		
Cars	250 Testa Rossa Sport	
	Engine: V-12 2953cc	
	Power output: 300 hp at 7500 rpm	
Victories:	Buenos Aires 1000 kms	P. Hill-Allison
	Le Mans 24 Hours	Gendebien-Frere
Ferrari World Sports Car Champions		
Production	250 GT, 250 GT Berlinetta, Spider California,	
	250 Spider California II, 410 SuperAmerica	

A dramatic photo of the Italian GP during which von Trips was killed when his Ferrari left the track and ploughed into the spectators crowding the banking along the Vialone straight.

1961

The previous season's preparations and the fact that the rival teams lacked competitive engines revived Ferrari's fortunes, as had been the case when the regulations were changed in 1952.

Right, the start of the Italian GP (10th of September) with Phil Hill, that season's World Champion, and Richie Ginther's Ferraris on the front row of the grid and the shirt-sleeved Ingegnere Carlo Chiti, the designer of the car, in the background.

Ferrari also adopted the mid-engine layout for its sports cars. Left, the presentation of the 246 P at Maranello.

The best results, however, were obtained with the classic TR 61. Below, the Rodriguez brothers' car that retired at Le Mans.

Formula 1 World Championship		
Cars	156	
	Engine: V-6 1481cc	
	Power output: 190 hp at 9500 rpm	
Drivers:	P. Hill, W. von Trips, G. Baghetti, R. Rodriguez,	
	R. Ginther, O. Gendebien	
Victories:	Dutch GP	W. von Trips
	Belgian GP	P. Hill
	French GP	G. Baghetti
	British GP	W. von Trips
	Italian GP	P. Hill
P. Hill	World Champion	
Ferrari	1st, World Constructors' Championship	

After the deaths of Castellotti and Musso, it was the turn of Giancarlo Baghetti in a semi-works Ferrari to keep the Italian flag in GP races, winning the French GP at Reims on his debut (2nd of July). Baghetti was the latest in a series of drivers to have gained experience in Formula Junior.

Pininfarina continued its series of styling exercises on the 400 Superamerica chassis, producing the third version of the Superfast, an analogous coupé known as the Aerodinamico (left) and the cabriolet with a hard-top (below), presented at the Geneva Motor Show.

Pininfarina also produced this prototype 250 berlinetta that Tavano and Baghetti drove at Le Mans.

World Sports Car Championship

Cars	246 P	
	Engine: V-6 2417cc, 270 hp	
	250 Testa Rossa	
	Engine: V-12 2953cc, 300 hp	
Victories:	Sebring 12 Hours	P. Hill-Gendebien (250TR)
	Targa Florio	von Trips-Gendebien (246S)
	Le Mans 24 Hours	P. Hill-Gendebien (250 TR)
	Pescara 4 Hours	Bandini-Scarlatti (250TR)
Ferrari	World Sports Car Champions	
Production	250 GTE, GT Berlinetta, Spider California, Coupé, 400 Superamerica, Superfast II	

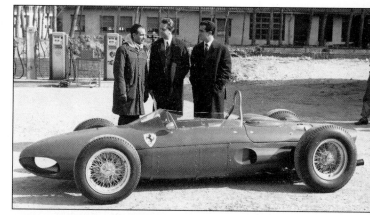

Above, John Surtees testing at Monza with the 286. The same car can also be seen here on the right. Ludovico Scarfiotti won the European Mountain Championship with a similar machine.

1962

The Formula 1 car was unchanged, but Lorenzo Bandini joined the team (seen above alongside Baghetti and Mairesse)

For the international GT championship Ferrari produced the all-conquering 250 GTO designed by Scaglietti who made use of Pininfarina's research into aerodynamics with the 250 Sperimentale the previous year.

G. CAVARA

With echoes of the frontal styling of the Sports and Formula 1 cars, Bertone presented this 250 GT (right) at the Geneva Motor Show. The car was penned by Giorgetto Giugiaro.

Pininfarina designed and produced the Ferrari GT 2+2 (or 250 GT/E) seen on the left in 1961, and was also responsible for two revised versions of the Superfast, the III and IV, both on the 400 Superamerica chassis (bottom)

Formula 1 World Championship
Cars   156
              Engine: V-6 1476cc
              Power output: 200 hp at 10000 rpm
Drivers: R. Rodriguez, W. Mairesse, L. Bandini, P. Hill, G. Baghetti
      Ferrari 18 pts. (6th, FIA Constructors' Championship)

Other competition cars
Cars   246 P
              Engine: V-6 2417cc, 278 hp
Victories: Sebring 12 Hours   Bianchi-Bonnier
              Targa Florio   Mairesse-Rodriguez-Gendebien
              Nürburgring 1000 kms   P. Hill-Gendebien
              Le Mans 24 Hours   P. Hill-Gendebien
              International Sports Prototype Championship winner
Cars   250 berlinetta
              Engine: V-12 2953cc, 300 hp
              International GT constructors' championship winner
Cars   196 SP
              Engine: V-6 1983cc, 210 hp
              European Mountain Championship winner L. Scarfiotti

Production   250 GTO, 250 Spider California, 250 GTE,
              GT Berlinetta, 400 Superamerica,
              250 GT Coupé Cabriolet, Superfast III, Superfast IV

Above left, Scarfiotti and Mairesse's 250 P that triumphed at the Nürburgring and right, the 250 Le Mans Stradale version of the same model. The obsolete tubular space-frame chassis of the F1 cars was abandoned in favour of a monocoque (above right, Surtees during the German GP), while the GTOs continued to dominate (below at Monza).

1963

The 250 GT/L berlinetta designed by Scaglietti (left and top right) and presented at Paris in 1962 continued to be marketed and no less than 350 examples were built in a little over two years. Pininfarina used the car as the basis for a special version with a nose that recalled the Superfast (top left), a model that itself was further modified (bottom).

Formula 1 World Championship		
Cars:	156	
	Engine: V-6 1476cc	
	Power output: 200 hp at 10200 rpm	
Drivers:	J. Surtees, W. Mairesse, L. Bandini	
Victories:	German GP	J. Surtees
	Mediterranean GP	J. Surtees
	Kyalami GP	J. Surtees
J. Surtees	22 pts (4th overall)	
Ferrari	26 pts (4th FIA Constructors' Championship)	

International Sports Prototype Trophy		
Cars	250 LM	
	Engine: V-12 2953cc, 310 hp	
Victories:	Sebring 12 Hours	Surtees- Scarfiotti
	Nürburgring 1000 kms	Surtees- Mairesse
	Le Mans 24 Hours	Scarfiotti- Bandini
Winner of the over two litres class		
Cars	196 S	
	Engine: V-6 1983cc, 200 hp	
Winner of the up to two litres class		
Cars	250 GTO	
	Engine: V-12 2953cc, 250 hp	
Winner of the over two litres class International GT Constructors Championship		
Production	250 Berlinetta GTO, 400 Superamerica, 250 GT 2+2, 250 GTL Berlinetta	

1964

A V-8 engine was developed allowing Surtees to win the F1 World Championship (left, at Monza), while Bandini raced the 6-cylinder (above at the Nürburgring) and the brand-new 12-cylinder boxer unit (below, in the colours of the North American Racing Team).

Formula 1 World Championship		
Cars	158, 156, 1512	
	Engine (158) V-8 1489cc	
	Power output: 200 hp at 10500 rpm	
Drivers:	J. Surtees, L. Bandini, L. Scarfiotti, R. Rodriguez	
Victories:	Syracuse GP	J. Surtees (158)
	German GP	J. Surtees (158)
	Austrian GP	L. Bandini (156)
	Italian GP	J. Surtees (158)
J. Surtees	40 pts World Champion	
Ferrari	45 pts Winner FIA Constructors' Championship	

The refusal of the authorities to homologate the 250 Le Mans in the GT category (above at Monza) induced Enzo Ferrari to abandon his status as official Italian entrant in protest and to entrust the cars to teams of other nationalities such as Luigi Chinetti's NART (see previous page).

Above the 330 P driven by Bandini and Surtees finished third overall at Le Mans behind the Ferraris of Guicet and Vaccarella and Bonnier and Hill. The GTO/64 was successfully used to defend the GT title from the assault of the American Shelby Ford Cobras.

International GT Constructors' Championship

Cars	275 P	
	Engine: V-123280cc, 320 hp	
Victories:	Sebring 12 Hours	Maglioli-Parkes
	Nürburgring 1000 kms	Scarfiotti-Vaccarella
	Le Mans 24 Hours	Guichet-Vaccarella
Ferrari International GT Constructors Champion, over two litres class		
Production	250 GTO/64, 250 GTL, 275 GTS, 500 Superfast,	
	330 GT 2+2, America, 250 LM, Superamerica	

Giovan Battista "Pinin" Farina (left) was responsible for the latest version of the Superfast (above) and the new 1964 Ferraris that were powered by the 3300cc 275 engine, the GTB (left) and the GTS (bottom right), and the four-litre GT 2+2 (bottom left).

1965

Bandini and Surtees, above at Monte Carlo, were unable to repeat the success of 1964, but the P2s (right, and below in the closed version prepared for Bandini and Biscaldi to drive at Le Mans) again managed to beat off the Ford challenge.

A production record of 740 in a year was achieved and alongside a new version of the 330 GT 2+2 (left), Ferrari decided to produce cars with medium-sized engines using the 6-cylinder Dino unit. Pininfarina extrapolated this Dino 206 (below left) and the 250 Le Mans Speciale (bottom) from the competition Dino (below right) that Scarfiotti drove to win the Mountain Championship.

Formula 1 World Championship

Cars		158 F1
		Engine: V-8 1489cc, 210 hp
		1512 F1
		Engine: V-12 1489cc, 220 hp
Drivers:		J. Surtees, L. Bandini, N. Vaccarella,
		B. Bondurant, P. Rodriguez
	Ferrari	26 pts (4th FIA Constructors' Championship)

International Sports Prototype Championship

Cars		330 P2
		Engine: V-12 3960cc, 410 hp
		275 P2
		Engine: V-12 3200cc, 350 hp
		275 LM
		Engine: V-12 3200cc, 320 hp
Victories:		Le Mans 24 Hours	Gregory-Rindt
		Monza 1000 kms	Guichet-Parkes
		Nürburgring 1000 kms	Surtees-Scarfiotti
		Targa Florio	Vaccarella-Bandini
International Sports Prototype Champion			

European Mountain Championship

Cars		Dino 166P
L. Scarfiotti Champion		

Production   250 LM, 330 GT 2+2, 500 Superfast, 275 GTB/GTS

Ferrari's twentieth anniversary season did not bring much racing success, in part due to Surtees leaving for Cooper-Maserati midway through the championship. In spite of Surtees and Parkes' victory in the Monza 1000 kms (right, below right and in the cut-away drawing) the P3 was beaten to the Sports Prototype title by the Fords. The Dino 206 (bottom left with Nino Vaccarella alongside) was beaten by the Porsches while in Formula 1 the 312 lost out to the Brabham despite Scarfiotti's victory at Monza.

1966

Left, The 3-seater 365 P with a central steering wheel that was produced in two examples for Gianni Agnelli and Luigi Chinetti. Below left, the 330 GTC that used the chassis of the 275 GTB and independent rear suspension.

The first version of the Pininfarina designed Dino 206 GT (below) was presented at the Turin Motor Show. The coachbuilder was also responsible for the 365 California cabriolet (bottom, left) that replaced the Superfast.

Formula 1 World Championship
Cars: Ferrari 312
                  Engine: V-12 2989cc
                  Power output: 360 hp at 10000 rpm
Drivers: J. Surtees, L. Bandini, M. Parkes,
                  L. Scarfiotti, G. Baghetti
Victories: Belgian GP   J. Surtees
                  Italian GP   L. Scarfiotti
        Ferrari   31 pts (2nd, FIA Constructors' Championship)

International Sports Prototype Championship
Cars: 330 P3
                  Engine: V-12 3967cc
                  Power output: 420 hp at 8000 rpm
Victories: Monza 1000 kms   Surtees-Parke
                  Spa 1000 kms   Scarfiotti-Parkes

Other competition cars
                  Dino 206 S   categoria sport 2000
                  275 LM
Production   330 GTC, GT 2+2, 275 GTB, GTB/C, GTS
                  500 Superfast, 365 California
Dream cars   Dino Berlinetta GT

1967

FIAT BUYS FERRARI

1976

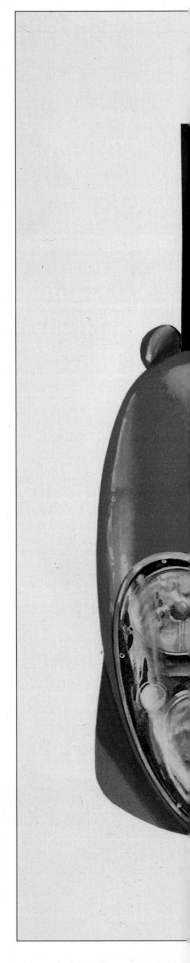

*T*he Maranello firm's racing commitments against increasingly competitive rivals in the F1 and sports prototype ca-

tegories seriously compromised its financial situation, and in 1967 just 706 cars were produced. Enzo Ferrari therefore offered the largest Italian automotive business the opportunity to buy a controlling share in his company, reserving the right to remain in charge of race management and President of the firm. This historic agreement was signed on the 18th of June, 1969, and as early as 1970 there was already a noticeable change in the Ferrari production philosophy. The classic V-12 engine was abandoned in favour of a 180° flat twelve unit, first in the 1970 F1 cars, then in the 1971 Sports Prototype and the 365 GT/4 BB Gran Turismo model introduced in 1973. From 1974 the firm's involvement in competition was gradually reduced to just the Formula 1 team. 1974 also saw the presentation of the new three-litre V-8 production engine installed in a transverse, central layout in the 308 GT/4 berlinetta. A two-litre version of this model was produced for the Italian market only as a means of avoiding taxation on large engines. The success of the new industrial strategy can be seen from the fact that 1,426 cars were produced in 1976 and 1,844 in 1972.

53

1967

The team's depression over the death of Lorenzo Bandini at Monte Carlo (right, with the race manager Franco Lini) was in some small part mitigated by the success of the 330 P4 (bottom during the Monza 1000 kms with Vaccarella-Muller who finished fourth, and below).

The definitive version of the Dino 206 GT was presented at the Turin Motor Show. It featured a central, transverse engine. The bodies were built by Scaglietti (left). Production of the Pininfarina 365 GT 2+2 (below left) also got underway and the car was to remain in the Ferrari catalogue until 1971. On the other hand, the 330 GTC went out of production after 600 examples had been completed. The photo below, right, shows the special version created by the Turinese coachbuilder who was also responsible for the styling exercise on the 206 S Competizione chassis (bottom).

Formula 1 World Championship		
Cars:	Ferrari 312	
	Engine: V-12 2989cc	
	Power output: 390 hp at 10800 rpm	
Drivers:	L. Bandini, L. Scarfiotti, C. Amon, M. Parkes,	
	J. Williams, A. De Adamich	
Victories:	0	
Ferrari	20 pts. (4th, FIA Constructors' Championship)	

International Sports Prototype Trophy		
Cars	330 P4	
	Engine: V-12 3967cc	
	Power output: 450 hp at 8000 rpm	
Victories:	Daytona 24 Hours	Amon-Bandini
	Monza 1000 kms	Amon-Bandini
	International Champions, over two litres category	

Other competition cars		
	Dino 1600	formula 2
	Dino 206 S	up to two litres category
Production	330 GT 2+2, Dino GT, 330 GTC, GTS, 275 GTB/4,	
	365 GT 2+2	
Dream cars	Dino berlinetta prototype coupé	

1968

This was a transitional year with no F1 wins (left and below left, Chris Amon) with the debut of the Dino-engined F2 driven by Tino Brambilla and an attempt to produce a Can-Am car with which to compete in the enormously popular American race series. (Below and centre left).

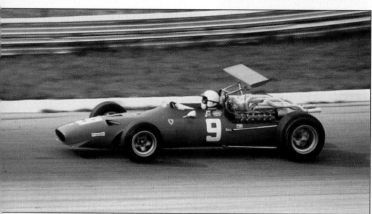

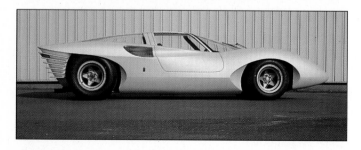

Ferrari did not take part in the Sports Prototype category races and the P4 served as the basis for Pininfarina's 250 P5 (above and right).

The three photos below show the 365 GTB/4 presented at Paris in 1968. The model was unofficially known as the Daytona in honour of the triumphant 1-2-3 success of the P4s at the American track in 1967. The car was homologated in the August of 1971 after the 500 examples required by the FIA had been constructed.

Pininfarina built this one-off prototype road car known as the P6 around a backbone girder chassis (left). The styling anticipated that of the future 308.

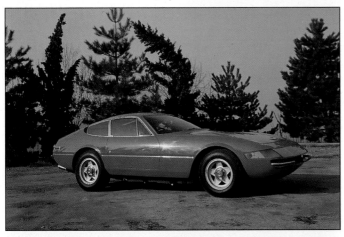

Formula 1 World Championship
Cars: Ferrari 312
                     Engine: V-12 2989cc
                     Power output: 410 hp at 10800 rpm
Drivers: J. Ickx, C. Amon, A. De Adamich
Victories: French GP   J. Ickx
        J. Ickx   27 pts. (4th overall)
        C. Amon   10 pts (10th overall)
        Ferrari   32 pts. (4th, FIA Constructors' Championship)

European Formula 2 Championship
Cars   Dino 166 F2
                     Engine: V-6 1500cc
                     Power output: 225 hp at 11000 rpm
        T. Brambilla 3rd overall in European Championship

Other competition cars
                     Dino 246 Tasmania, Can Am 612
                     212 E sperimentale

Production   365 GT 2+2, 330 GTC, GTS, 206 Dino GT,
                     275 GTB/4

Dream cars   250 P5, P6

1969 was another barren year for Ferrari in Formula 1 (right, testing at Modena with engineer Mauro Forghieri instructing Tino Brambilla).

1969

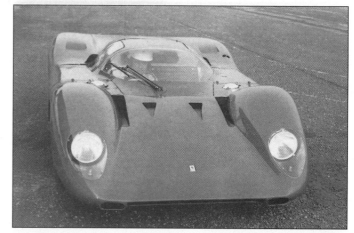

The Sports Prototype season was also unsuccessful with the new 312P proving to be exceptionally quick in qualifying but failing to translate this performance into race wins. Above, left, the Amon-Andretti 312 P at the Sebring 12 Hours (22nd of March) that was taken to second place overall and, right, the berlinetta version prepared for Le Mans. Schetty with the 212 E (right) won the European Mountain Championship, Ferrari's only title of the season.

In advance of the presentation of the 512 S race car, Pininfarina used it as the mechanical basis for this car characterised by extremely sophisticated aerodynamics developed in collaboration with the Polytechnic of Turin. Scaglietti began production of the Pininfarina-designed Daytona spider known as the 365 GTS/4 (below), while the Turinese coachbuilder itself produced this special version on the 365 GTB/4 chassis.

Formula 1 World Championship
Cars:		Ferrari 312
		Engine: V-12 2989cc, 435 hp
Drivers:		C. Amon, P. Rodriguez
	Ferrari	7 pts. (5th, FIA Constructors' Championship)

International Championship for Makes
Cars:		312 P
		Engine: V-12 2989cc, 410 hp
Drivers:		C. Amon, M. Andretti, P. Schetty, P. Rodriguez
	Ferrari	15 pts (4th overall)

Other competition cars
	166 Dino formula 2
	Engine: V-6 1593cc, 230 hp
	246 Dino Tasmania
	Engine: V-6 2404cc, 290 hp
Drivers:	C. Amon (Tasman Champion, 1969)
	212 E
	Engine: 12 boxer 1990cc, 300 hp
Drivers:	P. Schetty (European Mountain Champion)
	612 Can Am
	Engine: V-12 6221cc, 640 hp

Production	365 GT 2+2, Dino 206 GT, Dino 246 GT, 365GTB/4, 365 GTB/4 Spider Speciale, 365GTC/GTS

Left, Jacky Ickx at the Italian GP. In spite of four Grand Prix wins the Ferrari team (below, from left, Andretti, Ferrari, Giunti and Regazzoni) only succeeded in finishing second in the Formula 1 World Championship and the International Championship for Makes.

1970

New cars were introduced this season and the 12-cylinder boxer engine was adopted for F1 (below, left, in the hands of Ignazio Giunti at Spa). The endurance races were disputed with the 512 S homologated for the Sport category (below, right the car driven by Surtees and Schetty to third place in the Monza 1000 kms).

Pininfarina presented this futuristic dream car known as the Modulo and based on the 512 S mechanical platform (left) at the 1970 Geneva Motor Show. The 512 S was modified for the Le Mans 24 Hours with a lengthened tail and improved aerodynamics that favoured maximum speed on the long Les Hunaudières straight (centre and bottom).

Formula 1 World Championship

Cars	Ferrari 312 B
	Engine: 12 boxer 2991cc,
	Power output: 450 hp at 11500 rpm
Drivers:	J. Ickx, C. Regazzoni, I. Giunti

Victories:		
	Austrian GP	J. Ickx
	Canadian GP	J. Ickx
	Mexican GP	J. Ickx
	Italian GP	C. Regazzoni
J Ickx	40 pts (2nd overall)	
C Regazzoni	33 pts (3rd overall)	
Ferrari	52 pts (2nd, FIA Constructors' Championship)	

International Championship for Makes

Cars	512
	Engine: V-12 4993cc
	Power output: 580 hp at 8500 rpm
Drivers:	M. Andretti, I. Giunti, N. Vaccarella, C. Amon, J. Surtees, P. Schetty, A. Merzario, C. Regazzoni, J. Ickx, J. Oliver

Victories:		Sebring 12 Hours	Giunti-Andretti-Vaccarella
	Ferrari	37 pts (2nd overall)	

Production	365 GT 2+2, 365 GTC, 365 GTB/4, GTS/4, Dino 246 GT

The 312 B continued to be developed as the team searched for greater reliability and improved performance. Right, Clay Regazzoni before retiring from the Monte Carlo GP (23rd of May), followed by the car constructed by the former Ferrari driver John Surtees and driven by Rolf Stommelen.

1971

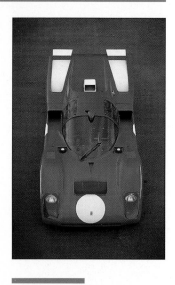

The 512 was further modified in a vain attempt to beat the Porsche 917s (top left and right with Manfredini and Gagliardi during the Monza 1000 kms) but greater efforts were concentrated on the development of the 312 PB with the F1 engine (right, driven by Ickx and Regazzoni in the Nürburgring 1000 kms) in view of the changes in the regulations for 1972.

1971
Formula 1 World Championship

Cars	Ferrari 312 B /312 B2
	Power output: 460 hp at 12000 rpm
Drivers:	J. Ickx, C. Regazzoni, M. Andretti

Victories:	South African GP	M. Andretti
	Dutch GP	J. Ickx

J. Ickx	19 pts (4th overall)	
C. Regazzoni	13 pts (7th overall)	
M. Andretti	12 pts (8th overall)	
Ferrari	33 pts (3rd, FIA Constructors' Championship)	

International Championship for Makes

Cars:	Ferrari 312 PB, Ferrari 512 M
	Engine (312 PB): 12 boxer 2991cc
	Power output: 440 hp at 11800 rpm
Drivers:	I. Giunti, A. Merzario, J. Ickx, C. Regazzoni, M. Andretti

Victories:	Kyalami 9 Hours	Regazzoni-Redman
Ferrari	26 pts (3rd overall)	

Production	512 M (tuning kit for 512 S)
	365 GTB/4, GTS/4, 246 Dino GT, 365 GT 2+2
	365 GTC/4

Ignazio Giunti, a specialist in the Buenos Aires 1000 kms, with Enzo Ferrari.

The 212 E (below) powered by the 12-cylinder boxer engine derived from the 1964 F1 unit was raced by Edoardo Lualdi in hillclimbs but achieved little of note. The 365 GT 2+2 was replaced by the 365 GTC/4 (bottom).

63

1972 was an indifferent F1 season for Ferrari. Forghieri's 312 B2s achieved a number of top-three placings but only one victory, in the German GP thanks to a fantastic performance by Jacky Ickx (right).

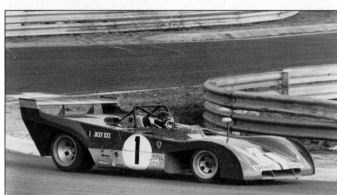

1972

Ferrari's warhorse for the Sports car championship was the 312 PB (left the cars driven by Ickx at Vallelunga and, below, Andretti at Sebring), designed by Mauro Forghieri. Formula 1 technology and exceptional drivers allowed the team to dominate the season.

Pininfarina completed the range of Ferrari road cars with a 2+2 destined for a clientele with less extreme demands in terms of outright performance (right). The 365 GT4 2+2 represented a valid alternative to the fast executive saloons available on the market.

Left, Tim Schenken during the Monza 1000 kms at the wheel of the 312 PB.
The 12-cylinder boxer engine was used in a production car for the first time with the launch of the 365 GT4 Berlinetta Boxer (below left) designed by Pininfarina. This was a variation on the mid-engined berlinetta theme developed with the 246 GT and GTS (below right).

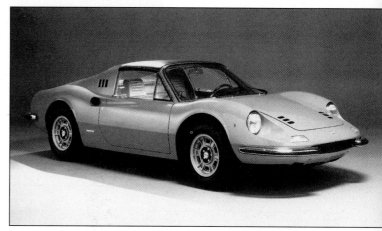

Formula 1 World Championship

Cars:	312 B2	
	Engine: 12 boxer 2991cc	
	Power output: 480 hp at 12800 rpm	
Drivers:	J. Ickx, C. Regazzoni, M. Andretti, N. Galli, A. Merzario	
Victories:	German GP	J. Ickx
	J. Ickx	27 pts (4th overall)
	C. Regazzoni	15 pts (6th overall)
	Ferrari	33 pts (4th, FIA Constructors' Championship)

World Championship for Makes

Victories:	Buenos Aires 1000 kms	Peterson-Schenken
	Daytona 6 Hours	Andretti-Ickx
	Sebring 12 Hours	Andretti-Ickx
	Brands Hatch 1000 kms	Andretti-Ickx
	Monza 1000 kms	Ickx-Regazzoni
	Spa 1000 kms	Merzario-Redman
	Targa Florio	Merzario-Munari
	Nürburgring 1000 kms	Peterson-Schenken
	Zeltweg 1000 kms	Ickx-Redman
	Watkins Glen 6 Hours	Ickx-Andretti
Ferrari	160 pts World Champions	

Production	246 Dino GT/GTS, 365 GT4 Berlinetta Boxer, 365 GTB/4, GTS/4 and 365 GTC/4 Competizione, 365 GTC/4

In line with the now universally adopted technical strategy Ferrari developed a monocoque chassis. The British specialist Thompson created the 312 B3. The marriage of the Maranello 12-cylinder engine and such a different chassis was problematical from the outset at Barcelona with Ickx (right).

1973

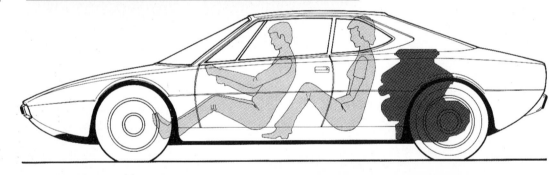

Ferrari also had a difficult season in the World Championship for Makes. The 312 PB (left) had to give second best to Matra in spite of revised weight distribution and aerodynamics.

Bertone was entrusted with the development of an unprecedented project: a mid-engined 2+2 baptised as the 365 GTB4. On the right, the unusual layout and below, the resulting car.

Formula 1 World Championship

Cars:	Ferrari 312 B2 / 312 B3
	Engine: 12 boxer 2991cc
	Power output: 490 hp at 12600 rpm
Drivers:	J. Ickx, A. Merzario
Victories:	0
Ferrari	12 pts (6th, FIA Constructors' Championship)

World Championship for Makes

Cars:	312 PB
	Engine: 12 boxer 2991cc
	Power output: 480 hp at 11500 rpm
Drivers:	A. Merzario, J. Ickx, C. Reutemann,
	B. Redman, C. Pace, T. Schenken, N. Vaccarella
Victories:	Monza 1000 kms Ickx-Redman
	Nürburgring 1000 kms Ickx-Redman
Ferrari	115 pts (2nd overall)

Production	365 GTB/4, 365 GTS/4, 365 GTB/4 Competizione, 365 GT/4 Berlinetta Boxer, Dino 246 GT, Dino 246 GTS, 365 GT/4 2+2

The work carried out during the previous season, a decisive change of direction in terms of the team management and the withdrawal from the World Championship for Makes all began to bear fruit. Lauda (below) took Ferrari back to the top step of the podium while Regazzoni, unfortunate at Monza (right), missed out on the World Championship by just 3 points.

1974

There were no significant changes to the Ferrari production range, but Pininfarina did produce this futuristic styling exercise known as the CR 25.

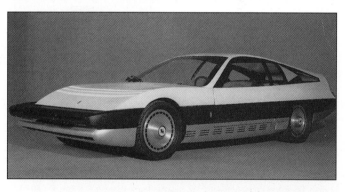

Formula 1 World Championship		
Cars:	312 B3 /74	
	Engine: 12 boxer 2991cc	
	Power output: 490 hp at 12600 rpm	
Drivers:	C. Regazzoni, N. Lauda	
Victories:	Spanish GP	N. Lauda
	Dutch GP	N. Lauda
	German GP	C. Regazzoni
C. Regazzoni	52 pts (2nd overall)	
N. Lauda	38 pts (4th overall)	
Ferrari	65 pts (2nd, FIA Constructors' Championship)	
World Championship for Makes		
Cars	312 PB/74	
	Engine: 12 boxer 2991cc	
	Power output: 480 hp at 11500 rpm	
	Did not participate	
Production	Dino 308 GT/4 Bertone, GT/4 2+2, 365 GT/4 Berlinetta Boxer, Dino 246 GT, Dino 246 GTS	

The development of the already very competitive 312 B3 included a major change with the adoption of the transverse gearbox, the new car thus equipped being known as the 312 T. It was a remarkable success and Lauda (centre, driving to victory in the French GP) and Regazzoni (bottom) won six championship Grands Prix and two non-championship events. Lauda was crowned as World Champion and Ferrari won the constructors' championship. Top, right, this shot reveals the twelve-cylinder boxer engine, the compact dimensions of the new transverse gearbox and the characteristic shape of the wings.

1975

A change in the F1 regulations led to a disappearance of the periscope-style air intakes and their replacement with two NACA ducts either side of the cockpit.

The appearance of the 312 T was otherwise unchanged but the latest version was known as the 312 T2. Right, Enzo Ferrari posing proudly with his two drivers Regazzoni and Lauda alongside the new T2 characterised by aerodynamic fairing in front of the front wheels and above all by the long-awaited number 1 assigned to the reigning World Champion.

Commercial pressures and the opportunity for purchasers in Italy to avoid heavy taxation led to the introduction of a 2000cc eight-cylinder engine fitted to the Dino GT4. The model was rebaptised as the 208 GT4 (bottom). However, the event of the year in terms of Ferrari production cars was the launch of the new mid-engined berlinetta destined to replace the 246 GT. Pininfarina's design was a perfect synthesis of the taut lines of the 365 BB and the curvaceous styling of the earlier model. It was named the 308 GTB (right) and in various forms remained in production for over a decade.

Formula 1 World Championship		
Cars:	312 T (Trasversale)	
	Engine: 12 boxer 2991cc	
	Power output: 495 hp at 12600 rpm	
Drivers:	N. Lauda, C. Regazzoni	
Victories:	Monaco GP	N. Lauda
	Belgian GP	N. Lauda
	Swedish GP	N. Lauda
	French GP	N. Lauda
	United States GP	N. Lauda
	Italian GP	C. Regazzoni
	BRDC International Trophy	N. Lauda
	Swiss GP	C. Regazzoni
N. Lauda	64.5 pts (World Champion)	
C. Regazzoni	25 pts (5th overall)	
Ferrari	72.5 pts (1st, FIA Constructors' Championship)	
Production	Dino 208 GT/4 Bertone, Dino 308 GT/4 Bertone, 365 GT/4 Berlinetta Boxer, 365 GT/4 2+2	

The 1976 season was positive in overall terms and only Lauda's dramatic accident during the German GP prevented him from winning his second World Championship.
Left, the Swiss driver Regazzoni, a Maranello stalwart, made a valid contribution to the team's retention of the Constructors' Championship.

Above left, the new version of the Berlinetta Boxer, now known as the 512 BB following an increase in cylinder capacity. Above right, the evolution of the 2+2 model now known as the 400 and supplied on request with an automatic gearbox. Right and below, the Rainbow: a Bertone styling exercise using the 308 GT4 mechanical platform.

1976

Formula 1 World Championship		
Cars:	312 T2	
	Engine: 12 cyl. 2991 cc	
	Power output: 500 hp at 12300 giri /min	
Drivers:	N. Lauda, C. Regazzoni, C. Reutemann	
Victories:	Brazilian GP	N. Lauda
	South African GP	N. Lauda
	USA West GP	C. Regazzoni
	Belgian GP	N. Lauda
	Monaco GP	N. Lauda
	British GP	N. Lauda
N. Lauda	68 pts (2nd overall)	
C. Regazzoni	31 pts (5th overall)	
Ferrari	83 pts (1st, FIA Constructors' Championship)	
Production	365 GT4 2+2, 365 GT4 Berlinetta Boxer, 308 GT/4 Bertone, 208 GT/4 Bertone, 308 GTB	
dream cars	Rainbow Bertone	

1977

Turbochargers for race and road

1986

Ferrari's fourth decade, 1977-1986, saw increasingly widespread adoption of the transverse central V-8 engine layout in the Ferrari Gran Turismo models. The power unit was available first in three-litre form, then as a two-litre for the Italian market only, and finally with an increased total displacement of 3200cc. Among the innovations worthy of mention were the adoption of four valves per cylinder and turbocharging. The commercial success of the new cars that were introduced led Ferrari to organise production in two factories, flanking the Maranello plant with another in Modena dedicated to the construction of bodies. In 1985 the company was employing 1,700 workers and production levels had reached 3,000 cars a year, around 80 percent of which were exported. In this period the Maranello firm concentrated its competition efforts on Formula 1, but following the triumphs of Niki Lauda in 1977 and Jody Scheckter in 1979, the team's run of success was interrupted with the adoption of the 1500cc turbocharged engines. Harvey Postlethwaite was hired in 1981 and Ferrari approached the 1982 season in a better frame of mind, but tragedy and bad luck destroyed the Italian marque's hopes of conquering the Drivers' championship. First came the death of Villeneuve, then Pironi's serious accident and finally Tambay's physical problems. Ferrari's victories in the 1982 and 1983 Constructors' World Championships were the last titles to be won in a ten-year period that concluded with the hiring of John Barnard as designer and the creation of a research and development center in England devoted to the creation of the single-seater for the 1987 season.

1977

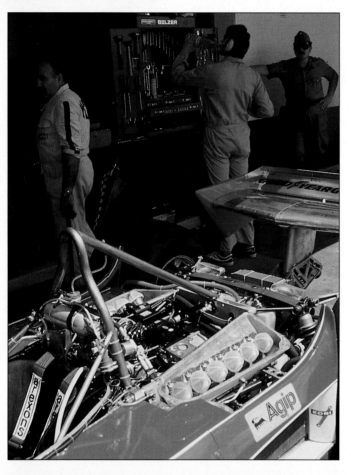

Further development of the 312 T2 brought Ferrari another drivers' championship, again through Niki Lauda, and a third consecutive constructors' championship thanks in part to the contribution made by newcomer Carlos Reutemann, an early winner in Argentina. Left, the glorious 12-cylinder boxer engine and, right, the born again Lauda racing at Long Beach.

IWith an eye to the future Pininfarina worked on a prototype based on the 308 GTB (below). As was usually the case at Maranello, the successful berlinetta was followed by an open-top version, the 308 GTS (on the facing page).

	Formula 1 World Championship	
Cars:	312 T2 /77	
	Engine: 12 cyl. 2991cc	
	Power output: 500 hp at 12200 rpm	
Drivers:	N. Lauda, C. Reutemann, G. Villeneuve	
Victories:	Brazilian GP	C. Reutemann
	South African GP	N. Lauda
	German GP	N. Lauda
	Dutch GP	N. Lauda
N. Lauda	72 pts (World Champion)	
C. Reutemann	42 pts (4th overall)	
Ferrari	95 pts (1st, FIA Constructors' Championship)	
Production:	308 GTB, 308 GT/4 Bertone, 208 GT/4 Bertone, 400 GT, 400 GT Automatica, 512 Berlinetta Boxer	
dream cars	Pininfarina exercise based on 308 GTB	

1978

Formula 1 World Championship

Cars:	312 T2		312 T3
	Engine: 12 boxer, 2991cc		
	Power output: 510 hp at 12400 rpm		
Drivers:	C. Reutemann, G. Villeneuve		
Victories:	Brazilian GP (312 T2)		C. Reutemann
	USA West GP		C. Reutemann
	British GP		C. Reutemann
	USA East GP		C. Reutemann
	Canadian GP		G. Villeneuve

C. Reutemann	48 pts (3rd overall)
G. Villeneuve	17 pts (9th overall)
Ferrari	58 pts (2nd, FIA Constructors' Championship)

Production	308 GTB, 308 GTS, 208 GT/4 Bertone, 308 GT/4 Bertone, 400 GT, 400 GT Automatica, 512 Berlinetta Boxer

The photos here show the nocturnal launch of the 312 T3. With this car and with the help of the new Michelin radial tyres, Reutemann and his new team-mate Gilles Villeneuve won four Grands Prix. Unfortunately for Ferrari this was the year of the genial ground effects Lotus 79 that with the aid of its innovative aerodynamics dominated the Maranello 12-cylinder cars.

With the adoption and development of the new aerodynamic concepts introduced in 1977 by Colin Chapman on the Lotus, the 312 T4 won both the drivers' and constructors' championships. Left, the famous sideskirts.

1979

On a triumphant day at Monza (previous page, bottom) Scheckter and Villeneuve destroyed their rivals, above all Laffite in the Ligier, the only real challenger for the championship title. Below, the two Ferraris running away from the field again, this time at Monte Carlo. Right, Villeneuve in the 312 T4: a legend in the making. Bottom right, Scheckter inspecting the 12-cylinder boxer engine designed by Forghieri.

Formula 1 World Championship

Cars:		312 T3	312 T4
		Engine: 12 boxer 2991cc	
		Power output: 510 hp at 12400 rpm	
Drivers:		J. Scheckter, G. Villeneuve	
Victories:		South African GP	G. Villeneuve
		USA West GP	G. Villeneuve
		Belgian GP	J. Scheckter
		Monte Carlo GP	J. Scheckter
		Italian GP	J. Scheckter
		USA East GP	G. Villeneuve
	J. Scheckter	51 pts (World Champion)	
	G. Villeneuve	47 pts (2nd overall)	
	Ferrari	113 pts (1st, FIA Constructors' Championship)	
Production		308 GTB, 308 GTS, 308 GT/4 Bertone,	
		400 GT, 400 GT Automatica, 512 Berlinetta Boxer	

Left, the usual photo with the drivers and the new car, the 312 T5 with Scheckter and Villeneuve. The season proved to be so disastrous that the team even practised at Imola with the brand-new 126 C with the 1500 cc turbocharged engine (bottom left).

1980

Above, two shots of the Mondial 8, the heir to the out of production 308 GT4, the mid-engined 2+2 layout of which it shared.

As well as the Mondial 8, Pininfarina presented the 400 Pinin: the first four-door Ferrari, it was based on the 400 GT. The three photos here highlight its main features, the concealed screen pillars and self-ventilating wheels.

Formula 1 World Championship	
Cars:	312 T5
	Engine: 12 boxer 2991cc
	Power output: 515 hp at 12400 rpm
Drivers:	J. Scheckter, G. Villeneuve
Victories:	0
J Scheckter	2 pts (19th overall)
G Villeneuve	6 pts (14th overall)
Ferrari	8 pts (10th, FIA Constructors' Championship)
Production	Mondial 8, 308 GTB/GTS, 208 GTB/GTS, 308 GT/4 Bertone, 400 GT, 512 Berlinetta Boxer
Dream cars	400 Pinin

Formula 1 World Championship

Cars:	126 CK	
	Engine: V-6 1496cc Turbo	
	Power output: 540 hp at 12000 rpm	
Drivers:	G. Villeneuve, D. Pironi	
Victories:	Monaco GP	G. Villeneuve
	Spanish GP	G. Villeneuve
	G. Villeneuve 25 pts (7th overall)	
	Pironi 9 pts (13th overall)	
	Ferrari 34 pts (5th, FIA Constructors' Championship)	
Production	308 GTB/GTS Iniezione, 208 GTB/GTS, 400i, 512 Berlinetta Boxer	

With the glorious 12-cylinder boxer engines having been abandoned, Ferrari F1 hopes were pinned on the 126 CK (right) and the horsepower of its turbocharged motor.
In spite of the arrival of the Frenchman Didier Pironi (above) the season was only saved by the heroics of Villeneuve. He scored memorable victories in Spain (top, leading Laffite's Ligier) and at Monte Carlo.

The new 126 C2 proved to be the car to beat in 1982: the engine, chassis and aerodynamics allowed the drivers to perform well from the very start of the season. Left, Villeneuve, 3rd at Long Beach and, below, Pironi, 1st at Imola.

1982

he death of Villeneuve at Zolder and Pironi's serious accident in Germany obliged Ferrari to bring in Tambay (right) and even Andretti, who had first driven for Ferrari back in 1969. The drivers' title went elsewhere but the team took the constructors' championship.

Formula 1 World Championship		
Cars:	126 C2	
	Engine: V-6 1496cc Turbo	
	Power output: 650 hp at 12000 rpm	
Drivers:	G. Villeneuve, D. Pironi, P. Tambay, M. Andretti	
Victories:	San Marino GP	D. Pironi
	Dutch GP	D. Pironi
	German GP	P. Tambay
D. Pironi	39 pts (2nd overall)	
P. Tambay	25 pts (7th overall)	
G. Villeneuve	6 pts (15th overall)	
M. Andretti	4 pts (19th overall)	
Ferrari	1st, Constructors' World Championship	
Production	208 Turbo, Mondial 8, 512i Berlinetta Boxer, 308 GTB/GTS Iniezione, 400i	

Two evocative portraits of Gilles Villeneuve, right, concentrating at the wheel and, below, thoughtful in the pits. What should have been the Canadian's year of triumph proved to be fatal. A misunderstanding with the German driver Jochen Mass during practice for the Belgian GP provoked the accident that cost the life of the best loved of all Ferrari drivers.

Formula 1 World Championship

Cars:	126 C2/C3		
	Engine: V-6 1496cc Turbo		
	Power output: 620 hp at 11500 rpm		
Drivers:	R. Arnoux, P. Tambay		
Victories:	San Marino GP		P. Tambay
	Canadian GP		R. Arnoux
	German GP		R. Arnoux
	Dutch GP		R. Arnoux
R. Arnoux	49 pts (3rd overall)		
P. Tambay	40 pts (4th overall)		
Ferrari	1st, Constructors World Championship		

Production	Mondial Quattrovalvole Cabrio,
	Mondial Quattrovalvole,
	308 GTB/GTS Quattrovalvole, 400i,
	512i Berlinetta Boxer, 208 Turbo

1983

The use of the turbocharged engine in Formula 1 encouraged Ferrari to introduce the technology to its road cars. the 308 berlinetta range was expanded with the launch of the 208 Turbo (right). The Mondial range also featured a new arrival, the Cabrio (top).
The arrival of the Frenchman Arnoux allowed the Formula 1 team to overcome the trauma of the loss of Villeneuve and win a total of 4 Grands Prix.

Eleven years after Merzario in 1973, an Italian returned to the wheel of a Ferrari: Michele Alboreto. The Milanese driver had proved his worth with Tyrrell and did not disappoint: he won the third race of the season in Belgium, and the Italian anthem was heard once again eighteen years after Scarfiotti's victory at Monza in 1966. Together with his team-mate Arnoux, took Ferrari to second place in the constructors' championship behind the uncatchable McLarens of Lauda and Prost.

This was an important year for Ferrari production cars with the launch of two new models with names evoking the glory years of endurance racing. Left, a detail of the 288 GTO destined for competition; below, two views of the Testarossa, heir to the 512 BB.

1984

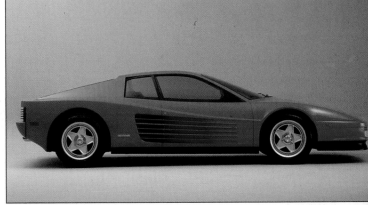

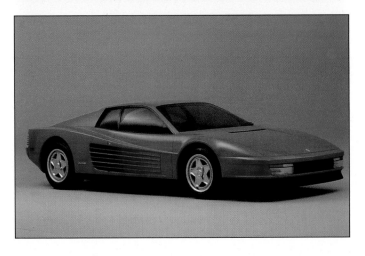

Formula 1 World Championship		
Cars	126 C4	
	Engine: V-6 1497cc Turbo	
	Power output: 730 hp at 11000 rpm	
Drivers:	R. Arnoux, M. Alboreto	
Victories:	Belgian GP	M. Alboreto
M. Alboreto	30.5 pts (4th overall)	
R. Arnoux	27 pts (6th overall)	
Ferrari	57.5 pts (2nd, Constructors' Championship)	
Production	288 GTO, 208 Turbo, 412i	
	308 GTB/GTS Quattrovalvole	
	Mondial Quattrovalvole	
	Mondial Cabrio Quattrovalvole	
	512i Berlinetta Boxer	

Alboreto (left), now the number 1 driver, was able to match Prost and his McLaren up to mid-way through the season thanks to a truly competitive car, and dominated drivers of the calibre of Senna, Rosberg, Lauda, Mansell and Piquet. With the season underway Johansson (below, with Alboreto) replaced Arnoux in car number 28. The motives were never explained but the Swede silenced the sceptics when in just his second race he swept into the lead in the San Marino GP at Imola and sent the tifosi into raptures.

1985

A true cabriolet was seen once again at Maranello with the launch of the open-top Mondial (below) designed for those clients unsatisfied with the removable roof panels of the GTS models produced until then.

Formula 1 World Championship

Cars	156 / 85	
	Engine: V-6 1496cc	
	Power output: 800 hp at 11500 rpm	
Drivers:	M. Alboreto, R. Arnoux, S. Johansson	
Victories:	Canadian GP	M. Alboreto
	German GP	M. Alboreto
M Alboreto	53 pts (2nd overall)	
S Johansson	26 pts (7th overall)	
R Arnoux	3 pts (19th overall)	
Ferrari	82 pts (2nd, Constructors' Championship)	

Production	Testarossa, 288 GTO, 328 GTB/GTS
	Mondial Quattrovalvole
	Mondial Quattrovalvole Cabrio, 412, 208 Turbo

A limp end of season and the extraordinary progress of the new Honda engines powering the Williams machines meant that the F1 car had to completely redesigned. Left, the new F186 that, with the same drivers as the previous year, defended the honour of Maranello. Unfortunately, however, Alboreto and Johansson (below) were able to play only minor roles in what was the hardest fought championship of recent years. Four drivers were in the hunt up to the last race with Alain Prost eventually taking the title.

Bottom, over thirty years after Ascari's experience, Ferrari once again investigated the possibility of an American adventure at Indianapolis with a car built to the US regulations.

1986

Formula 1 World Championship	
Cars:	F1 86
	Engine: V-6 1496cc Turbo
	Power output: 850 hp at 11500 rpm
Drivers:	M. Alboreto, S. Johansson
Victories:	0
M. Alboreto	14 pts (8th overall)
S. Johansson	23 pts (5th overall)
Ferrari	37 pts (4th, Constructors' Championship)
Production	Mondial 3.2, Mondial 3.2 Cabrio, 328 GTB/GTS 412, Testarossa, GTB Turbo, GTS Turbo, 288 GTO Formula Indy project

1987

Back to the roots

1996

In spite of the death of Enzo Ferrari in 1988, this ten-year period was marked by a return to the philosophy that the Drake himself had preached at Maranello. The crisis in the Middle East contributed to this change in direction, as did the fact that part of the very identity of the Ferrari marque had been lost with the development of an overly diversified product range. The business strategy adopted by Luca Cordero di Montezemolo, the new President of Ferrari from December, 1991, consisted in the consolidation of the elite

image of the Ferrari marque, and the abandonment of the mirage of the 5,000 cars per annum production total (an objective that had almost been reached in 1991), with production being pegged at a maximum of 3,000 examples a year. These cars would find a guaranteed market among enthusiasts throughout the world. 12-cylinder engines once again became synonymous with Ferrari, both in the classic 65° V configuration and the 180° boxer layout. Use of the sparkling 90° V-8 was restricted to the 348 and subsequently the 355. Following the GTO and the Testarossa the company continued to use model names such as the F 512 TR that established ties with Maranello's glorious sporting tradition. A tradition that was also revived with the creation of a one-marque race series for the F 348 and then the F 355 models. This brought back memories of the 1950s and 1960s when Ferrari's sporting clientele dominated racing throughout the world with their 250 GT berlinettas. The last act in this dramatic return to the company's roots was represented by the 1996 launch of new cars characterized by classic front-engined architecture, albeit updated to take advantage of the latest driving aids.

1987

he latest change in the F1 personnel involved the departure of Johansson and the arrival of the talented Austrian Gerhard Berger (right). Following a fairly slow start to the season brightened by the occasional good placing, he won the last two Grands Prix.

In spite of great effort and dedication Michele Alboreto (below) was unable to emulate the success of his team-mate. On the facing page, top, the powerful 6-cylinder engine with the two lateral turbochargers.

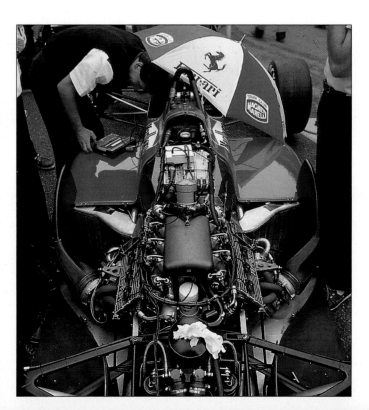

1987 represented a fundamental stage in the history of the marque as the Scuderia Ferrari celebrated its fortieth anniversary. The event was celebrated with the presentation of an ultra-high performance berlinetta that was created as a road car but had obvious competition potential: the F40.

The avant-garde technology, the dramatic lateral air intakes and above all the conspicuous rear wing were all features that attracted the attention of the marque's sporting clientele.

Formula 1 World Championship
Cars   F1 87
                 Engine: V-6 1496cc Turbo
                 Power output: 880 hp at 11500 rpm
Drivers: M Alboreto, G Berger
Victories: Japanese GP   G. Berger
                 Australian GP   G. Berger
      G. Berger   36 pts (5th overall)
      M. Alboreto 17 pts (7th overall)
      Ferrari   53 pts (4th overall)

Production   Testarossa, 412, GTB/GTS, Mondial 32
                 Mondial 3.2 Cabrio, GTB Turbo; GTS Turbo

These three views of the F40 reveal the dramatic styling in all its glory. The rear wing was the only controversial feature, but in this case Pininfarina had more than merely aesthetic matters to consider. In order for the almost 480 horses produced by the twin-turbo V-8 (facing page) to be fed through to the asphalt efficiently a stylistic compromise had to be reached. Nonetheless, the success of the car is reflected in the total number built: 950 examples over five years.

1988

1988 proved to be another indifferent year of the F1 team. Berger (left) and Alboreto (below) enjoyed only one day of triumph at Monza where, favoured by a collision between Senna and a driver he was lapping, they finished first and second.

Formula 1 World Championship
Cars:	F1 87/88
	Engine: V-6 1496cc
	Power output: 650 hp at 11500-rpm
Drivers:	M. Alboreto, G. Berger
Victories:	Italian GP G. Berger
G. Berger	41 pts (3rd overall)
M. Alboreto	24 pts (5th overall)
Ferrari	65 pts (2nd, Constructors' Championship)
Production	F 40, 412, Testarossa, 328 GTB/GTS, GTB Turbo
	GTS Turbo, Mondial 3.2, Mondial 3.2 Cabrio
14th August	Enzo Ferrari dies

13517

Enzo Ferrari died at Modena on the 14th of August. On the facing page a Young Enzo Ferrari, a works driver with Alfa Romeo at the Targa Florio, leaning on the bonnet of an Alfa Romeo RL. Top left and right, a smiling Ferrari in the pits and an equally jovial Commendatore during an official dinner. below left and right, Enzo Ferrari with Luca Cordero di Montezemolo during the traditional end of year press conference and during a rally while inspecting an Alfa Romeo P3 equipped
with twin rear tyres in 1934.

15th of August, 1934, Coppa Acerbo at Pescara. A thoughtful Enzo Ferrari between the Mercedes W 125 of Rudy Caracciola and the Alfa Romeo P3 of Achille Varzi entered by the Scuderia Ferrari on behalf of the Milanese manufacturer.

1989

This season the team tackled the World Championship without its founder at the helm for the first time. Honouring the memory of Enzo Ferrari was an extra stimulus for the drivers (Mansell, the new arrival, and Berger) and the engineering staff who presented a brand-new an extremely innovative car with a gear change mounted on the steering wheel (soon imitated by all the other teams). It was powered by a 3.5-litre, V-12 engine in accordance with the new Formula 1 regulations.

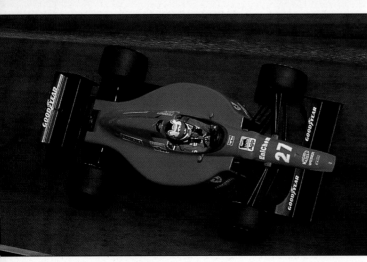

Formula 1 World Championship			
Cars:	F1 89 (640)		
	Engine: V-12 3497cc		
	Power output: 665 hp at 13200 rpm		
Drivers:	G. Berger, N. Mansell		
Victories:	Brazilian GP		N. Mansell
	Hungarian GP		N. Mansell
	Portuguese GP		G. Berger
	N. Mansell	38 pts (4th overall)	
	G. Berger	21 pts (7th overall)	
	Ferrari	59 pts (3rd, Constructors' Championship)	
Production	Mondial T, Mondial T cabrio, 328 GTB, 328 GTS 412, Testarossa, F 40, GTB Turbo, GTS Turbo		
dream cars	Pininfarina Mythos		

On the production side the company presented the latest versions of the Mondial (bottom), the Mondial T, coupé and cabriolet. The most interesting features of these cars were technical: longitudinal 3405 cc engine with transverse gearbox and electronic dampers.
Left, the new Pininfarina masterpiece, the Mythos. As with all the other dream cars produced over the years, this was purely a styling exercise with no production potential.

With the signing of reigning champion Alain Prost (below) the legen-
dary number 1 returned to the nose
cone of a Ferrari. Misunderstandings
with his team-mate Mansell (right)
and a highly controversial collision
with Ayrton Senna in the last Grand
Prix meant Prost had to settle for
second place in the championship
behind the Brazilian.

1990

Right, the streamlined shape of the 641 F1, a development of the F1 89 designed the previous year under the supervision of John Barnard at the brand-
new technology centre specially created for him in Great Britain.

After passing through its last incarnation known as the 328, the glorious 308 was replaced by a new "small" Ferrari, the 348 TB. Accompanied by the usual open-top version, the TS, it was based on the well proven Mondial T mechanicals. The most eye-catching styling elements were the lateral air intakes that resembled smaller versions of those of the Testarossa. Particular attention was paid to safety: the 348 TB was the first Ferrari to be fitted with ABS.

Formula 1 World Championship					
Cars	641 F1			British GP	A. Prost
	Engine: V-12 3497cc			Spanish GP	A. Prost
	Power output: 710 hp at 13800 rpm			Portuguese GP	N. Mansell
Drivers:	A. Prost, N. Mansell		A Prost	71 pts (2nd overall)	
Victories:	Brazilian GP	A. Prost	N Mansell	37 pts (5th overall)	
	Mexican GP	A. Prost	Ferrari	110 pts (2nd, Constructors' Championship)	
	French GP	A. Prost			
			Production	348 TB, 348 TS, 412, Testarossa, F 40	

1991

Formula 1 World Championship	
Cars:	642
	Engine: V-12 3497cc
	Power output: 740 hp at 14700 rpm
Drivers:	A. Prost, J. Alesi, G. Morbidelli
Victories:	0
A. Prost	34 pts (5th overall)
J. Alesi	21 pts (7th overall)
G. Morbidelli	0.5 pts (24th overall)
Ferrari	55.5 pts (3rd, Constructors' Championship)
Production	348 TB, 348 TS, 412, Testarossa

The arrival of Alesi (top right) did not appear to be congenial to the perplexed Alain Prost (top left). The more powerful version of the 12-cylinder engine was unable to make up for the deficiencies of the 642 chassis. Even Prost (right) with all his undoubted technical and tactical skill was able to do little with the car. The stormy climate that had been created within the team and the forthright opinions expressed by Prost culminated in his sacking. Gianni Morbidelli replaced him for the remaining races of the season.

1992

Prost's place was taken by another Italian. Following Alboreto as a Ferrari works driver came Ivan Capelli, top left and centre at Monte Carlo and below at Monza. However, the F92 A characterised by unique aerodynamics designed by J. C. Migeot proved to be difficult to develop. Neither Alesi (top right) nor Capelli obtained significant results, the later being replaced by Larini.

Formula 1 World Championship		
Cars:	F 92 A	
	Engine: V-12 3497cc	
	Power output: 745 hp at 14700 rpm	
Drivers:	J. Alesi, I. Capelli, N. Larini	
Victories:	0	
	J. Alesi	18 pts (7th overall)
	I. Capelli	3 pts (12th overall)
	Ferrari	21 pts (4th, Constructors' Championship)
Production	512 TR, 456 GT, 348 TB, 348 TS	

On this page: three views of the new 512 TR. The parentage of the old Testarossa is very clear. The new wheels and the more aggressive frontal treatment did not interfere with Pininfarina's unmistakable design.

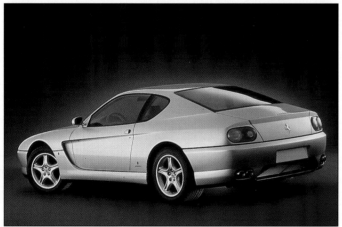

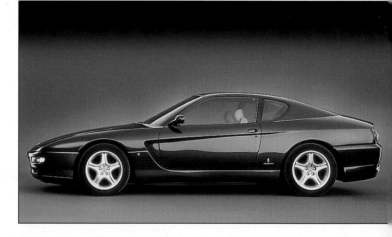

The 412 had also been pensioned off and the status of the most recent front-engined Ferrari was taken on by the 456 GT. This page shows four views of Pininfarina's latest 2+2. Whilst boasting extremely luxurious trim and finish, the car did not relinquish anything of the traditional Ferrari sporting character, being powered by a V-12 engine producing over 440 hp.

Yet another disappointing F1 season. Not even the return of the Austrian Berger (below) managed to revive the Maranello fortunes. The sporting event of the year was the launch of the Challenge 348, the first one-marque race series promoted by Ferrari. Clients could take to the tracks with their own cars, simply adopting the obligatory safety systems and making a few minor modifications (right).

Below, right, the 348 cabriolet destined principally for the American

1993

Formula 1 World Championship

Cars:	F 93 A	
	Engine: V-12 3497cc	
	Power output: 730 hp at 13500 rpm	
Drivers:	G. Berger, J. Alesi	
Victories:	0	
	J. Alesi	16 pts (6th overall)
	G. Berger	12 pts (8th overall)
	Ferrari	28 pts (4th, Constructors' Championship)

Ferrari Challenge 348

Cars:	348 TB Challenge
Production	348 TB, 348TS, TR, 456 GT

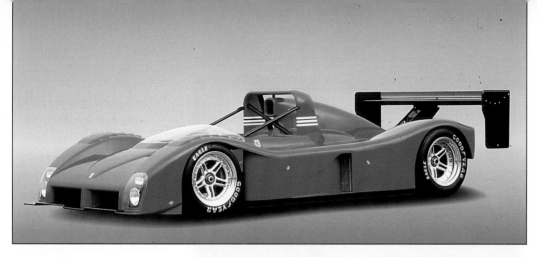

Left, the 333 SP. Following an interval of twenty years Ferrari made an official return to endurance racing. The chosen championship was the IMSA series in the USA. The regulations permitted the naturally aspirated 3997 cc to be used in a carbon-fibre chassis. The cars and all the necessary equipment for the arduous series that included races at Daytona and Sebring were acquired by private entrants.

The still young 348 went out of production to be replaced by the 355 (below, centre and bottom left) with a similar technical specification. In effect the car was a development that exalted the pros and eliminated most of the cons of its predecessor. The F512 M (bottom right), the last version of the Testarossa, was also worthy of note.

Victory at last! Berger (above) won the German Grand Prix, favoured by the retirement of the front runners.

1994

Formula 1 World Championship

Cars:	412 T1	
	Engine: V-12 3497cc	
	Power output: 780 hp at 15000 rpm	
Drivers:	G. Berger, J. Alesi, N. Larini	
Victories:	German GP	G. Berger
G. Berger	41 pts (3rd overall)	
J. Alesi	24 pts (5th overall)	
N. Larini	6 pts (14th overall)	
Ferrari	71 pts (3rd, Constructors' Championship)	

IMSA Championship

Cars:	F 333 SP
	Engine: V-12 3997cc
	Power output: 600 hp at 11500 rpm
Ferrari Challenge	
Cars	348 Challenge
Production:	F 355, F 512 M
	456 GT

With the same drivers being retained, the F1 team tackled the new FIA regulations specifying engines with total displacements of below 3000 cc. Right, J Alesi on the track.

1995

For the first time the very wealthiest Ferrari clients were able to purchase something very close, in terms of technology, to a Formula 1 machine. The F50, produced in open and closed versions (right), used a V-12 engine developing 520 hp (below), a chassis in composite materials and electronically controlled suspension. The driving position could be fully adjusted, including the pedal box. The Pininfarina coachwork featured a large rear wing and sophisticated underbody aerodynamics providing a Cx factor of 0.372.

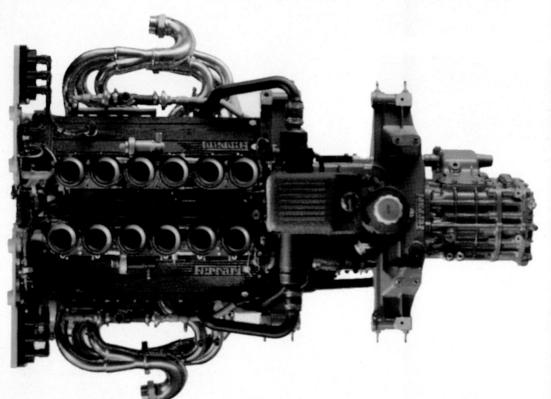

Formula 1 World Championship		
Cars:	412 T2	
	Engine: V-12 3000cc	
	Power output: 730 hp at 17000 rpm	
Drivers:	G. Berger, J. Alesi	
Victories:	Canadian GP	J. Alesi
	J. Alesi	42 pts (5th overall)
	G. Berger	31 pts (6th overall)
	Ferrari	73 pts (3rd, Constructors' Championship)

IMSA Championship	
Cars:	F 333 SP
	Engine: V-12 3997cc
	Power output: 600 hp at 11500 rpm
IMSA Champions 1995	

Ferrari Challenge	
Cars:	F 355
Production:	F355 spider, F355
	456 GT, F 50

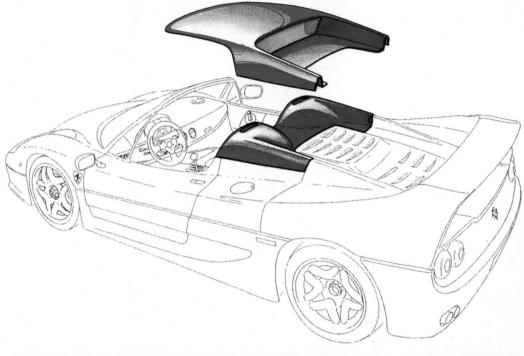

All change at Ferrari. New car (right, being unveiled for the first time) and new driver: the twice World Champion Schumacher (bottom left, and centre at the wheel) the kingpin of the new team rebuilding programme.

Bottom, the F 310 built around a brand-new V-10 engine had a familiar appearance thanks to the pontoon-style air intakes first seen in the ill-fated F92 A. Fortunately the similarities ended here.

1996

The Irishman Eddie Irvine had the unenviable task of playing second fiddle to Schumacher with no hope of avoiding frequently unkind comparisons. Below, "Schumi" at work. Remarkably he scored three wins in a season in which the domination of the Williams-Renault appeared otherwise absolute.

The latest car in the Ferrari stable is this 2-seater, front-engined berlinetta, the F 550 Maranello. this is the first time that the home of the Prancing Horse has been commemorated in the name of one of its products. Top, right, note the long bonnet, a typical feature of the berlinettas of the Sixties. The rounded styling also echoed classic Ferraris of the past. However, below the skin lies the most advanced competition technology: 485 hp at 7000 rpm, variable geometry intake manifolds, 6-speed gearbox, electronically controlled suspension, ABS and more; all helping this car to reach a maximum speed of 320 kph in complete safety.

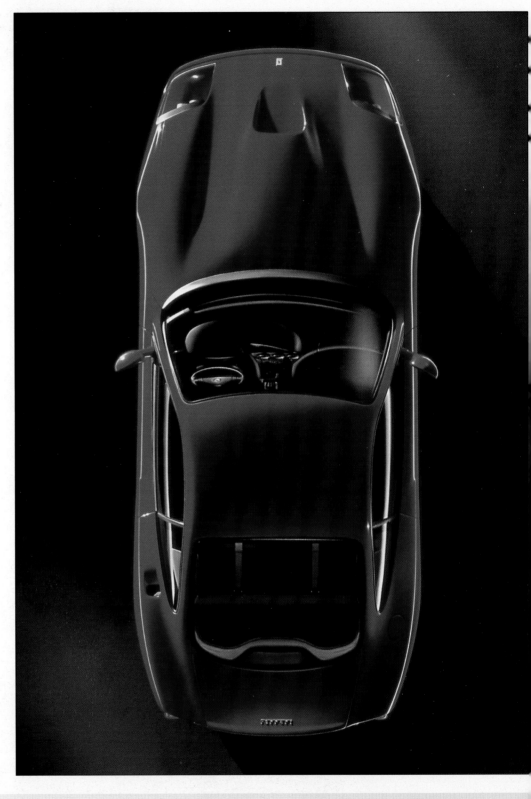

Formula 1 World Championship				Ferrari	70 pts (2nd, Constructors' Championship)
Cars:	F 310			IMSA Championship	
	Engine: V-10 3000cc			Cars:	F 333 SP
	Power output: 715 hp at 16000 rpm				Engine: V-12 3997cc
Drivers:	M. Schumacher, E. Irvine				Power output: 600 hp at 11500 rpm
Victories:	Spanish GP	M. Schumacher			227 pts (2nd, IMSA Championship)
	Belgian GP	M. Schumacher		Ferrari Challenge	
	Italian GP	M. Schumacher		Cars:	F355
M Schumacher	59 pts (3rd overall)				
E Irvine	11 pts (10th overall)			Production:	F550 Maranello, F50, F 355

Further views of the F 550 Maranello that allow us to appreciate the styling features and the luxurious interior upholstered in leather. Right, a view revealing the sophisticated aerodynamic underbody designed to provide downforce and lower wind resistance.

INDEX